The
Timescapes
of John Fowles

The
Timescapes
of John Fowles

H. W. Fawkner

Foreword by John Fowles

Rutherford ● Madison ● Teaneck
Fairleigh Dickinson University Press
London and Toronto: Associated University Presses

Associated University Presses
440 Forsgate Drive
Cranbury, NJ 08512

Associated University Presses
25 Sicilian Avenue
London WC1A 2QH, England

Associated University Presses
2133 Royal Windsor Drive
Unit 1
Mississauga, Ontario
Canada L5J 1K5

Library of Congress Cataloging in Publication Data
Fawkner, Harald William, 1946–
  The timescapes of John Fowles.

  Bibliography: p.
  Includes index.
  1. Fowles, John, 1926–   —Criticism and inter-
pretation. 2. Time in literature. I. Title.
PR6056.085Z66 1983   823'.914   82-48606
ISBN 0-8386-3175-4

Grateful acknowledgment is made to John Fowles and Little, Brown and Company for permission to quote from *The Magus: A Revised Version,* © 1965, 1977 by John Fowles; *The French Lieutenant's Woman* © 1969; *Daniel Martin,* © 1977 by J. R. Fowles Ltd.; *Mantissa,* © 1982 by J. R. Fowles Ltd.; *The Ebony Tower,* © by J. R. Fowles Ltd.; *The Collector,* © 1963, by John Fowles; and The Aristos, © 1964, 1968, 1970 by John Fowles; to Monthly Review Press for *Studies and Further Studies in a Dying Culture* by Christopher Caudwell, © 1971; to the University of California Press for *Time in Literature* by Hans Meyerhoff; to Laurence Pollinger and the Estate of John Cowper Powys for *Owen Glendower;* to Macdonald & Co. (Publishers) Ltd. for *A Glastonbury Romance* by John Cowper Powys; to Warner Bros. Inc. for lyrics from *Talkin' World War III Blues;* to A. D. Peters & Co. Ltd. and Random House for *Bricks to Babel,* © 1980 by Arthur Koestler; to Plenum Publishing Corporation for *The Integrated Mind* by Michael S. Gazzaniga and Joseph E. LeDoux; to Granada Publishing Ltd. for *Hemisphere Function in the Human Brain* by J. G. Beaumont and S. J. Dimond; to S. Karger A. G. for "Neuroevolutionary Mechanisms of Cerebral Asymmetry in Man" by Joseph E. LeDoux (figure); to Academic Press for "Time and Consciousness" by Richard A. Block, in *Aspects of Consciousness,* Volume 1, and to Penguin Books Ltd and Mr. Martin Gardner for *The Ambidextrous Universe* © Martin Gardner, 1964, 1969, 1979.

Printed in the United States of America

To Pia

Contents

*When a finger points at the moon
only a fool looks at the finger.*

Foreword by John Fowles

Though I am fortunate in the amount of study that has been devoted to my work, this is one of the few times it has been approached in a way that particularly interests me personally. I have a perhaps irrational dislike of the usual placing-and-marking context that seems congenial to so many teachers of literature: the fussing over "influences" and position in the league, as if the most important thing is pinning the poor writer on a genealogical map, or filing him in the right pigeonhole. I think of this as the pedagogic method, since it inevitably reduces its subjects to the status of pupils in a class—with echoes of the stock phrases of the school report ("should try harder," "some progress this year") always close behind the learned strictures and bouquets.

I write fiction very much to discover myself through texts—more precisely during the process of writing them—and very little to stake a claim on the flagrant quicksand of contemporary reputation. Studies like Dr. Fawkner's, that help me discover, even where I may disagree, are much more to my taste. My fictions are far more experiments than anything else—that is, in search of something, or things, always beyond the outward narrative and themes. This is a main reason why I find that writing, except on one or two superficial technical levels, does not get easier as I grow older; and why I have changed direction so often in the past, in orthodox literary terms.

In my own view all novelists share one common, if often largely unconscious, driving force: and that is a sense of loss, or at any rate of insufferable incompleteness, a deprivation we then habitually blame on the real world around us. This world is so wrong, so inadequate and unimaginative, that we must speak, and correct and supplement it. Such hubris explains the often absurdly misleading public masks novelists wear, and their marked bias toward realism of presentation (not least by setting their work in an imaginary past); and equally their fondness for playing puppet-master to their own creations—what I once called the godgame. Our eternal and most feared rival is the writer of the world that is the case. All novels are implicitly blasphemous, in challenging *that* gentleman's (or lady's) universally well published, and publicized, *oeuvre*.

Novels may also be seen, without exception and even when set in the future, as salvage operations. Of course what is to be recovered and repaired can vary immensely, but always at the heart of it lies a sense of loss—and one the novel can never truly remedy, though it may assuage it in part. I have argued elsewhere that this seemingly tragic (an adjective many writers secretly cherish in their self-pitying image of themselves) failure, or inability to recover all one wants, is really so much petrol in our psychic engines—and is also why novel-writing appears to be so markedly obsessive an activity. The truth is that if we ever did, by some miracle, recover our loss (in psychoanalytical terms, gain both intellectual and emotional insight into why we are as we are), we should be dead as novelists. If politics is the art of the possible, novel-writing is quite certainly the art of the impossible. Deep down we are much closer to pathological gamblers than pathetic martyrs crucified on a failure to win.

One constant component, perhaps the profoundest, of this fertile loss must be our inability to "conquer" or reverse time; in that, of course, we are joined by the rest of the human race. We cannot even re-create the past as it truly was, however hard and painstakingly we try, let alone literally make it other than it was. Nor can we create it as it will be, however percipiently we guess. All we can do is to give, by the dubious stratagem of inventing a past that never was, a more or less successful parody of how such a past might have been. But this doomed attempt is easily redeemed, inside the writer's secret self, by the wicked pleasure of creating a succession of mythical presents outside the historical series of presents that constitute the "real" past. (Most serious exponents of our sister profession in science, the historians, would not, I think, claim that they can do much better, once they leave documented hard facts for interpretation of them.)

There may be nothing divine whatever in the published fiction; there is always something divine (or time-escaping) in its creation. It is curious that so few novelists have ever spoken of this sweetest pleasure in the act of writing. Perhaps it is because writing is already quite sufficiently narcissistic, without this worst narcissism of all; or perhaps because the *written* product—the published book—only too often appears as time-bound, as crushed by Marvell's "wingèd chariot," as poor Prometheus on his rock.

But there is no doubt that the experience of *writing* fiction (however bad the written result in the outside world's eventual eyes) takes place in another and timeless world, and that this comes close to a universal yearning among all human beings. Even the simplest and shortest act of literary text, as brief as a haiku, is a surreptitious bid for immortality, or freedom from ordinary time. There was a vogue among art students a few years ago for throwaway or "disposable" art—the creation deliberately made not to last. It is significant that the idea received no sympathy at all from even the most avant-garde literary theorists.

I have long believed that this perhaps special ability of the word to help us escape from time (both in facilitating the escape and in sharing it) is as important a factor for the reader as for the writer. The reader is just as eager, if not more eager, to escape from linear or "clock" time, even though it is only aboard someone else's poem, novel, whatever it may be. What helps especially in sharing the experience is undoubtedly the imprecision of the word, as opposed to the once-and-for-all accuracy of the visual image. Such an image requires very little collaboration in the mind that receives it. A word demands a great deal; it is never the destination, merely a signpost in its general direction; and whatever transient physical, psychological, or moral body that destination finally acquires owes quite as much to the reader as to the writer. I have always refused to read my work in public for this reason; for fear that my voice and presence will color and distort this very peculiar relationship established between two minds by mute print alone.

The adventure of escaping scientific or clock time, the "real" onward-ticking now, underlies all our appreciations of the great literature of the past; and defines most of what we seek in the smallest literature of the present. All fiction, from the noblest to the basest, from Homer to the clumsiest pulp-market pornography, is first a private act, then a public offer, of escape from the surrounding world. It is one strong reason why fiction (novel or play) has always been so disliked by puritans of all persuasions, from extreme conservatives to extreme Marxists; and so appreciated by those who suffer from the world that is. Fiction is a perennial anarchist to all those bigots who believe that anything that distracts from final political, social, or religious aims must be dangerous, if not positively evil. It is society as state that wants us eternally spitted upon the minute-hand, denying past and future, those nonpresent fields of consciousness where we all become writers of fiction, at least in our own minds.

This capacity for transport "out of time" is, needless to say, largely governed by the skill with which an imaginary present (in past or future) is evoked. Dialogue is perhaps the most important instrument of that evocation for novelists, and this explains why we have such an ancient love-hate relationship with playwrights. Their art gives them immediate access to an eternal present. Never mind that Aeschylus or Shakespeare are dated by archaic circumstance, setting, language; when their characters speak, they are eternally now, inalienably in the narrative present. Something about the narrative past of most prose fiction has always seemed dark and dead to me. Verisimilitude and custom require it; it is also a defeat, an admission that a disguise is needed to achieve the illusion. It is true that most readers unconsciously translate the narrative past (or "past definite") on the page into a narrative present in the mind; I quite often "slip" tenses like this when I write first drafts, without noticing it till I reread.

This obsessive pursuit of timelessness, of an eternal present, (deeply rooted, I believe, in buried recollection of the time-free primal relation between mother and infant), is also a moral problem for most novelists, made worse by the necessarily long and solitary nature of the fiction-writing process. It can be used only too easily to justify a withdrawal from real time—the real travails and troubles of contemporary society. As Sartre claimed with Flaubert, the novelist retreats to the safe middle-class haven of "writer," and so effectively castrates any chance of becoming other than he has elected to be. He cannot quite get off on the plea that the said travails and troubles are his theme; the pen may be mightier than the sword, but no pen ever manned a barricade, or marched.

In *Daniel Martin* I symbolized this retreat as the "sacred combe," wishing to distinguish it from the more familiar ivory tower, with its suggestion of lifeless preciosity. But I have long had to realize that I live in a state of almost perpetual fugue from the present around me, and not only when I am writing. Even with old friends, or people with whom one ought no doubt to be all ears and attention, such as interviewers, I rarely feel fully present. Other dialogues, other answers, both remembered and fresh-imagined, accompany every real one; and other faces, other places. It is only when I am writing, in fact, that I can safely feel fully present, a reasonably whole identity.

Many would say that the ability of the novel to help people escape present time—and circumstances—for a few hours is a quite sufficient justification in itself, and has no need of the artistic and moral bonus we expect from great art. None the less I suspect that this comparative freedom to wander in time is a major cause of the characteristic neurosis of my profession, manic depression. A pragmatist would say we deserve no better for living an illusion; and trying to maintain that it is more real than reality. I have been accused of "making readers work"; giving them different endings to choose from, leaving moral dilemmas unresolved, using words most will have to look up in a dictionary, and so on. I regard this as trying to share the guilt, on my side; of not liking my capacity to lull.

But having, out of duty toward the always quarreling socialist side of my mind, put that question mark against the escapist side of the novel for the novelist himself, I confess I can think of worse sins and defects, and especially in this stage of world history. I have been called an existentialist, but I am essentially a pagan. Like every other being, I am here to enjoy life, and to help others enjoy it, and *now*. The ideal future worlds envisioned by communism and capitalism seem to me equally worthless, and I also believe that their proponents in power, both East and West, demand an atrocious present price from the rest of us in behest of their respective dreams. I cannot see anything evil in the chance to escape, if only briefly, from a real world as foolish, unjust, and imperfect as ours.

Even more importantly I think it is high time we liberated ourselves from the narrow blinkers imposed on us by the notion, both social and scientific, of time as an inexorable onward machine, a clock whose face we must constantly watch and respect and obey from the moment we first go to school. Psychological time, as every novelist can vouch, is enormously richer and more complex. . . and more pleasurable. I am well aware that all artists are privileged in being able to create and live in a variety of times, metaphorical equivalents of the different *tempi* of the composer; and that countless social and economic factors render such a life impossible except for this fortunate few. But while there may be an eternal bar between artists and nonartists in terms of natural ability, I can see none as regards a deeper understanding of life through a deeper understanding of time . . . I would almost say, a greater playfulness with time. This is one of the "things," behind outward theme and story, that I have always tried to say in my novels.

Perhaps the most interesting literary experiment of the recent past has taken place not in Paris or America but in China. The attempt there to suppress all art that does not remorselessly direct attention to present social needs and ends has conspicuously failed; as perhaps it was especially bound to, given the particularly delicate relationships with time demonstrated by the ancient Chinese poets. If there is one thing worse than escapism, it is surely the excessive politicization of time . . . decreeing that mankind must never leave the actual biological present.

I would like to close by quoting some passages from a letter I wrote to Dr. Fawkner when I first read his study.

"Fiction-writing is an intrinsically diachronic business, using the word in its linguistics sense: only to be undertaken and analyzed that way. Attempting to synchronize very varied pasts (make them emotionally equi-present, structurally equipoised, and so on), as I did in *Daniel Martin,* can't really (for me) be presented as some 'higher' reality, only as a sort of consolation. Various synchronisms you point out came to me (inasmuch as any of this comes very consciously, if at all) from cinema technique: cross-cutting, so-called jump-cutting. Years ago I analyzed my dreams in some detail, and found cinema techniques had clearly reached that level, even panning and traveling. I'm sure that historically the cinema techniques could largely be in turn derived from ancient literary ones (even as far back as Homer), but it seems to me that the vividness of the demonstration made this far more than a disguised feedback, perhaps because the unknowable unconscious is structured and 'writes itself' by images also—is wordless, in short. I recently saw the extraordinary six-hour version of Abel Gance's *Napoleon,* and was very struck by this aspect—its dreamlike, image-chaotic force, surging up behind the 'conscious' art. (The film also makes one realize how much was lost by the introduction of sound into the medium.)

"I suspect that this notion of an unconscious that constitutes itself by images alone, that is prelinguistic (and perhaps uncontaminated by clock-time, without any chronology at all), explains many word-handling problems that writers have and think of as clumsiness, faults of effort, knowledge, etc.—when the real problem is the Trojan Horse deep inside their own camp, though of course the 'offer' of it is one they can't refuse . . . as the real Trojans might have.

"I don't of course know if I am right in assuming that the unconscious is timeless (in the strict sense, without time, or chronology) as well as wordless. A certain kind of word-defying experience I have with nature I also class as timeless in this sense. I see it much more as a kind of everyday trick of conscious suppression of time than anything mystical; not an entry into a more 'real' world, as so many would suppose it, but into an alternative (or alternating, as in current) one, a fictional one in some ways. Most of us have this experience at command as children. I can see it happening in my three-year-old granddaughter, who is staying here at the moment. She stares at some minute event in the garden, a spider making its web, seeing it for the first time; the latter is the elision I hope for myself—seeing-for-the-first though it is chronologically the ten thousandth. This experience is of course easier to achieve when it really is, even at my age, a first one. It is also, with nature, a diachronic experience, that is, also an apprehension of endless repetition, timeless in the other sense. There are many passages in my books where I have tried to reproduce this both synchronic and diachronic affect before things or events; and usually failed, given what sometimes seems to be the active hostility of words at being dragooned into expressing what can only be felt, not described. A novelist must cherish all his ages, perhaps his child self most of all; the cost is that he will always be in exile from his society, above all from the society of his contemporaries. Most of mine seem increasingly older than I am to me, in every ordinary social and cultural sense.

"What I like (in personal experience) is in fact the interaction of 'timeless' time and ordinary time. It is an essential part of the meaning and pleasure of the event 'outside' time that it is transient, ephemeral, clock-devoured. This may lie behind my liking for various freakish time-coincidences I have installed in fiction: some need to lock scientific and emotional reality together in outwardly irrational ways (as Pasternak did, brilliantly in my view, in *Dr Zhivago*) or at least to remind the reader that art deals with different orders of reality than science.

"I know this sort of thing distresses many readers; they see it as destroying an illusion, betraying reality, and so on. But 'reality' begs countless questions. It is certainly a betrayal of real*ism*, yet strictly mimetic realism (being endlessly true to life) has always seemed to me the lowest form of literature—even in its greatest practitioners, like Zola—and finally true to life only in the most superficial and photographic sort of way; indeed untrue to life, in most others. Art has a very limited respect for any absolutes besides those of beauty and moral truth. It laughs at clocks and chronologies; so also, I believe, would an intelligent human society."

John Fowles, 1982

Note on the Text

I wrote this book after reading Fowles's novels. There was no rapport with Fowles, and I deliberately avoided reading critical works on Fowles so as to be able to approach his fiction with a free and unbiased mind. I do not regret having chosen this strategy. Without my knowing it Fowles happened to read a tentative introduction to my first manuscript. At his request I sent him the entire typescript. This did not include the three last chapters of this book. I soon began to daydream about the structure of human time and came to read J. T. Fraser's *Of Time, Passion, and Knowledge* (1975). This gave me the idea of a hierarchy of temporalities. The countless works on time were interesting (and difficult), but they did not seem to be able to account for the patterns of human time suggested by Fowles's fiction.

Communicating bilaterally with both John Fowles and Dr. Fraser, I was quite surprised at this time to discover that Fowles was about to attend the ISST workshop on time supervised by Dr. Fraser at Bellagio, Italy during the summer of 1981. In August 1982 Dr. Fraser paid me a visit in Sweden. During his three-day stay our different paradigms were tested against one another. Dr. Fraser expressed the feeling that my three temporalities—then named *subtemporality, nootemporality,* and *transtemporality*—were in fact subdivisions of his own *nootemporality* (from *noetic:* of the intellect, purely intellectual). We agreed to call my middle temporality *quotidian time.*

This book is not a study of time in Fowles. It is a study of Fowles with a definite organizing principle: temporality. The present project is therefore disidentified from a handful of journalistic introductions to the Fowlesian landscape. These surveys contain a vast amount of very useful information, but they tend to lack an organizing principle or to favor one that is sequential rather than structural. They fall outside the limits of scientific investigation, if by "scientific" we mean something more profound

than mere surface accuracy in the collection of biographical
and bibliographical data, some mode of exploration that goes
beyond the detective work required to determine "influences."

Unfortunately, these discursive overviews (Barry Olshen's
handy monograph being a notable exception) do Fowles quite a
lot of damage. The main reason for this is that in fiction the
whole is infinitely more than a mere summation of parts. A
multileveled vision is not a collection or sequence of independent perspectives; therefore criticism is not a question of breaking down as many doors as possible, but of spending time and
energy on finding a master key.

A perpetuated flaw is derived from the entirely false notion
that all Fowlesian statements cohabit a single dimension of discourse: quotes from the novels are forced into a kind of egali-
tarian rapport with maxims in *The Aristos* or even with
"explanations" in letters. When such thresholds of functional
relevance are ignored the metaphysical shallowness of interpretation becomes truly stunning. In addition a number of loose
concepts are used, each a blurred kernel with an aura of incompatible satellites: "progress," "freedom," "will," "humanity,"
"selfhood," "time"—chameleon words which tend to twist
themselves into contradictory pockets of meaning, and which
do not really help to clarify anything in analysis. Like the worn-
out Freudian categories these words are fast becoming just
about as useless as the medieval tetrads of elements and tem-
peraments, or the jargon of alchemy. When we say "freedom,"
do we mean freedom from tyranny and restrictions or freedom
from the chaos of laissez-faire? These are mutually exclusive.
When we say "naturalism," are we thinking of the stance in-
troduced by Zola, or are we simply suggesting something
vaguely associated with John Fowles's interest in ornithology
and wildlife conservation? There is a slight difference! When
discussing Fowles's "liberalism" are we in fact looking at his
socialism? If so, are we defining this "socialism" as social democracy, democratic socialism, Marxian socialism, or Marxist socialism? In Marx "socialism" is the transitional rule of the masses
prior to the "communism" of the classless utopia, the final
emancipation of man; in totalitarian bureaucracies it is something rather different. When we say "nausea," do we mean
Sartrean nausea (a distinctly metaphysical concept associated
with existentialist anguish of a very particular quality), or do we
just mean the general contemporary sense of futility? How can

we speak of "selfhood" without considering the multiplicity of incompatible selves; of Sarah's "ovulation" without seeing her as a node in the structure of the text rather than as an objectified acquaintance to be inspected by the amateur gynaecologist?

The fact that the languages of physics and mysticism are becoming indistinguishable suggests that we are now close to the limits of language. The verbal pigeonholes, the streams of discrete units in the text, are becoming the mirage fabric of space-time sheets beyond which loom dazzling zones of non-conceptual experience, interpenetrating mazes of psycho-energetic fields that make civilization look like a sensory deprivation chamber and the city culture of *Homo consumens* like the world line of a somnambulist. Into these realms I cannot take the reader, for this is a scientific investigation—not a step to Buddhahood.

This, however, does not mean that there is no connection between the curvature of space-time and the curvature of fiction-reality, between Einstein's view of time as relative to its frame of reference and the maya of Charles Smithson's trifurcated life, the apertures to elsewhere in Miles Green's amnesia, the retrocausality of Conchis's metatheater, the quaint zero-dimensionality and undulating nothingness of the anti-novel.

I have no yogic knowledge, no experience of hallucinogens, no competence within the field of physics. When discussing dextrotemporal explosions of consciousness I am therefore not thinking in terms of wheels of psychic energy in oriental charkas, bubbles in the quantum foam, or gradations of spinning stargates in a one-electron universe. In defining the meteorology of consciousness I am not evolving some esoteric abracadabra, some elaborate, pseudointellectual hocus pocus. Instead I am trying to get *away* from subjectivism and arbitrariness—from "psychoanalysis" with all its fantastic complexes, castrations, and anal-sadistic arabesques. As Erich Fromm has so brilliantly demonstrated in his *Greatness and Limitations of Freud's Thought* (1980), the Freudian hierarchy (including its grotesque view of woman) is to a large extent a projection of the class structure to which Freud belonged. The human mind has become a sort of Upstairs/Downstairs mansion with inherent domestic conflicts to be controlled from the "top." There are of course treasures of insight in Freud, but in the wake of some of

his patriarchal distortions of consciousness, temporal paradigms tend to emerge in which serial time is seated in pontifical
control of all other human temporalities. In a descending ladder of significance to utter "timelessness" (a kind of original sin,
it would appear) these unruly alternative temporalities are
looked upon as infantile or feminine threats to a sober, masculine, businesslike temporality in control, asserting its
hegemony, *its superior intelligence.*

In this book I question that superiority and that intelligence:
I discuss the patriarchal self-assertion of sinistral time (levotemporality), the nature and validity of its imperialism, the projections (mostly unconscious) of its will to power. John Fowles's
fiction is, in my view, a subversion of the pontifical paradigms
of time and consciousness; his novels are assertions of alternative modes of structuring human experience. Herein lies his
richness, his elusive complexity, his attraction for the intelligent
adult sensing the trap of modern time but unable to verbalize it.
Herein lies also Fowles's inaccessibility, his estrangement from
modes of literary inquiry based on patriarchal models of consciousness, time, and discourse.

The facts (the units and patterns of human experience
translated into fiction by Fowles) do not fit into the patriarchal
paradigms of temporality now available. If they did, I would
not have to hypothesize other, new paradigms. Strangely, the
temporal pattern that the facts *do* suggest implies a basic hori-
zontality in temporal awareness, an *equality* of temporal moods
in which the masculine and feminine aspects of time are basically interdependent entities in a dynamic dualism. To avoid
misunderstanding I must therefore point out that the two temporal models in this book are vertical (chapter 10) and horizontal (chapter 12) projections of a single three-dimensional spiral
which, for obvious reasons, I have had to translate into two
separate diagrams.

Quotations are from the Little, Brown and Company editions
of the novels. For *The Aristos* I have used the 1970 New American Library edition. For this work and for *Mantissa* references
within parantheses are to sections; in the other works numbers
within parantheses refer to chapters. Quotations from *The Magus* are from the revised version. In comparing the British and
American versions of the texts I have found only minor devia-
tions—mostly in spelling. There is one exception: in chapter 36
of *The French Lieutenant's Woman* "Ralph Leigh" has become

"Ralph Wood." I should like to point out that the first epigraph for chapter 12 of that novel is from Marx's *Economic and Philosophic* (not "Political") *Manuscripts*.

The various chapters in *Daniel Martin* have been numbered as follows:

1   The Harvest
2   Games
3   The Woman in the Reeds
4   An Unbiased View
5   The Door
6   Aftermath
7   Passage
8   The Umbrella
9   Gratuitous Act
10 Returns
11 Tarquinia
12 Petard
13 Forward Backward
14 Breaking Silence
15 Rencontre
16 Crimes and Punishments
17 Catastasis
18 Jane
19 Beyond the Door
20 Webs
21 A Second Contribution
22 Interlude
23 Hollow Men
24 Solid Daughter
25 The Sacred Combe
26 Rituals
27 Compton
28 Tsankawi
29 Westward
30 Phillida
31 Thorncombe
32 In the Orchard of the Blessed
33 Rain
34 A Third Contribution

Acknowledgments

I extend gratitude to John Fowles for his handsome contribution and authentic involvement; to Dr. J. T. Fraser, founder of *The International Society for the Study of Time,* for intellectual challenge, witty enthusiasm, and reckless generosity; to Professor Gunnar Sorelius and Mr. Thomas Yoseloff for promoting this project; to Professor Claes Schaar for most vital assistance and critical limpidity in the final phases of research; to David Treadwell, Malcolm Forbes, Barbro Kinnwall, Mavis Fawkner, and Nicholas Fawkner for technical assistance; to Professor Birgit Bramsbäck for caring advice and valuable suggestions; to Professor Alvar Ellegård for efficient scrutiny of the introductory chapter; to Donna Ostraszewski and Donald Yelton for editorial coordination; to Pelle Tivenius for friendship and crystallization; to Linda Fawkner for affectionate impishness; to Christina Eriksson for esoteric fluorescence; to my grandparents Thomas and Elizabeth Wood of Arnos Grove for a home in the wilderness; to Robin Fawkner (with his silver arrows) for twinklings in the greenwood.

For She whom the ancients named Cybele is in reality that beautiful and terrible Force by which the Lies of great creative Nature give birth to Truth that is to be.

Out of the Timeless she came down into time. Out of the Un-named she came down into our human symbols.

Through all the stammerings of strange tongues and murmurings of obscure invocations she still upholds her cause; the cause of the unseen against the seen, of the weak against the strong, of that which is not, and yet is, against that which is, and yet is not.

John Cowper Powys, *A Glastonbury Romance*

The
Timescapes
of John Fowles

1 Introduction

If no one asks me what time is, I know what it is; if I wish to explain it, I know not.

St. Augustine

"Now girl number twenty," said Mr. Gradgrind. "You know what a horse is."
Charles Dickens, *Hard Times*

A hologram is a three-dimensional photographic image developed with a laser. Every minute part contains the blueprint for the whole. A holographic representation of a clock can be tilted and viewed from different sides, but the organization of information in the hologram is such that the whole clock is always there, even when viewed from behind. If you cut the clock in half, you have two clocks, not two half-clocks. To get half-clocks you would have to surrender the superior organizing principle of the holographic transparency.

Looking at the dramatic split-brain data of neuropsychological hemisphere research, the critic may easily be tempted to say that time exists in the left cerebral lobe and timelessness in the right. In 1974 Jerre Levy makes a clear-cut statement which today looks like a rash generalization: "The right hemisphere synthesises over space. The left hemisphere analyses over time. . . . The right hemisphere perceives form, the left hemisphere, detail. The right hemisphere codes sensory input in terms of images, the left hemisphere in terms of linguistic descriptions. The right hemisphere lacks a phonological analyser; the left hemisphere lacks a Gestalt synthesiser."[1]

In early correspondence with John Fowles (1981) I mailed a copy of a *New Scientist* article in which it is claimed that the hemispheres of the human brain may not be so specialized after all, since full hemispherectomy (surgery completely removing left or right brain) seems to lead to remarkable recovery no

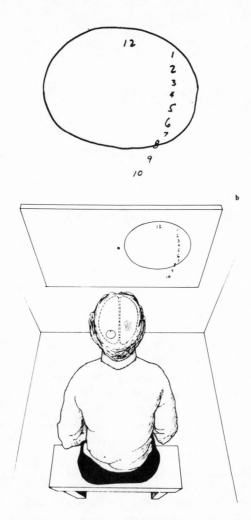

When presented with a circle and asked to draw in a clock face, a patient with inferior parietal lobule lesion in the right hemisphere placed all the numbers on the right side in a linear sequence (a). She was then asked to choose between her clock and a more typical exemplar, and she selected hers as the best clock to tell time with. Yet when her clock was presented directly to her left hemisphere through her right visual field (b) she immediately commented: "What a funny clock. The numbers are all on one side." When asked to draw a clock, seconds later, she again placed all the numbers on the right side and was again unconscious of the aberration. Here, the patient's behavior suggests that the inferiority of the left hemisphere is manipulo-spatial rather than visual. In a wider neurocognitive context, however, the drawing would seem to illustrate some of the more profound dislocations of consciousness outlined in the present study. From Joseph E. LeDoux, "Neuroevolutionary Mechanisms of Cerebral Asymmetry in Man," *Brain, Behavior and Evolution* 20 (1982): 199.

matter which lobe is left in the skull.[2] At the same time new reports suggest most interesting correlations between left-handedness, cerebral dominance, gender, lateralization (degree of hemisphere specialization), autoimmunity, and developmental learning disorders.[3]

It is not really vital for us to await the outcome of the psychobiological controversy, for it is still quite clear that we really do have two distinct and incompatible cognitive repertoires.[4] The two cerebral blueprints may be strongly tied to the hemispheres or to the degree of lateralization (specialization) of the two lobes; on the other hand the correlation may be quite insignificant. The fact remains that we still have two main competing cognitive repertoires. For the sake of convenience I shall call them "left" and "right." I do not think we should think of the cerebral lobes as parallel computers in alternating control. Instead we should think of the mind as a television set with two channels: each channel functions within the whole set, not half the set. So while it is very foolish to say that there is a channel to the left and a channel to the right, it is not foolish to say that there is a button to the left and a button to the right.

What has this got to do with literary criticism and the fiction of John Fowles? Just about everthing. In Fowles's *Mantissa* the female protagonist is a neuropsychologist. But this is very marginal. What is really important is that the metaphysical and ethical problems raised by the Fowlesian plot are the very metaphysical and ethical problems raised by the results from split-brain tests. While the New York neuropsychologists M. S. Gazzaniga and J. E. LeDoux challenge the hasty conclusions of some of their colleagues and of their own research, they recognize the existence of incompatible cerebral subsystems:

> The last implication of this model that we would like to consider surfaces right on the question of the nature of personal responsibility. Most of our social institutions are built on the notion that man is personally responsible for his actions, and implicit in that statement is a notion that man has a unitary nature embodied in the self. What are we now to do with that view, given the possibility that multiple selves exist, each of which can control behavior *at various moments in time?* . . .
>
> We are faced, it seems, with a new problem in analyzing the person. The person is a conglomeration of selves—a sociological entity. Because of our *cultural bias toward language*

and its use, as well as the richness and flexibility that it adds to our existence, the governor of these multiple selves comes to be the verbal system. Indeed, a case can be made that the entire process of maturing in our culture is the process of the verbal system's trying to note and eventually control the behavioral impulses of the many selves that dwell inside of us. (my italics)[5]

What outstanding neuropsychologists discuss tentatively in a speculative appendix is in Fowles elaborated in the complex texture of an entire body of fiction.[6]

It is also clear here that having the two cerebral systems in simultaneous duplication creates opposite extremes. The merged channels on the television screen of the mind may show nothing but the electronic blizzard of Cronus devouring his children. Yet at the opposite extreme from the interference problems of learning difficulties there is the multi-perspectival potential of cerebral synchronization displayed in Leonardo da Vinci's mirror-writing.[7]

There is nothing strange in Homo sapiens having two distinct cognitive styles. Indeed, it would be very strange if our species did *not* have two incompatible cerebral repertoires.

Considering the enormous complexity of the brain I think it is highly unlikely (in fact quite impossible) that the individual, healthy adult *ever* reverts to a cerebral subsystem corresponding to some earlier stage of evolution. Such units of earlier and inferior complexity cannot possibly dwell intact within the brain, superimposed by subsequent "layers" of mental sophistication. There are surely no hidden "geological" strata in the mind—no fossils that can be magically reanimated as soon as we happen to depart from the upspeeded flux of technological hypertime. Nor is it very likely that the two cognitive styles of man developed as the hominids split up into the subpopulations of hunters and nonhunters,[8] for even hunters spend most of their time not hunting; and even in the hunt only a small amount of time is devoted to the actual chase with its very different requirements for top speed processing of perceptual data and high frequency coordination of manipulospatial complexes.

All hunters need two cerebral styles (not left and right brain, but certainly two distinct cognitive repertoires): one for the long existential vistas in which *nothing* happens; another for those minutes (sometimes seconds, sometimes hours) when *everything* happens. Survival depends in the first phase on the imaginative, creative-associative ability to fight off monotony; in the second phase on the manipulative ability to eat and not be eaten. The selective mechanisms of evolution will therefore clearly favor individuals with the dual capacities for imaginative potentials within the monotonies of sensory deprivation and discriminative potentials within the frenzies of sensory over-stimulation. When discussing human time in fiction or else-where it is therefore most essential to appreciate the planetary rhythm of the animal kingdom to which we belong. On the savannah the shudders of fear that run through the grazing herds are interruptions, not states of being. Early man spent most of his time in comparative peace, in a torpor of physical inertia which his mental coding operations were evolved to in-terpret as something different from boredom. At closer exami-nation it will be found that *The French Lieutenant's Woman* catches the pattern of this existential rhythm which has been that of animal life for hundreds of millions of years as that of the Victorian age. I shall discuss this later; here I wish to call attention to the way in which the Fowles novel is structured to mirror and also reject the contemporary inversion of this rhythm—today the hectic now of an artificially accelerated tem-porality has reduced the contemplative mainland of the cere-bral atlas to an offshore island of quaint and redundant significance. The collective insanity of our age may well express the inability of the mind to cope with such a drastic reorienta-tion.

While the character types discussed by neuropsychologists are often little more than humanized guinea pigs or laboratory rats, the human characters of modern fiction display the psy-chological depth of living men and women. The traces left in the novel by the "events of inner experience" that Roger Sperry discusses in his Nobel lecture may therefore be quite as il-luminating as laboratory results in our attempts to define the nature of cerebral gearing in man.

Fowles's ambidextral mind has the ability to twist a plane of polarized experience clockwise ("time") or counterclockwise ("timelessness"). In the 1968 preface to *The Aristos* he states that "*the dividing line between the Few and the Many must run through each individual, not between individuals.*" This suggests an inter-nalized view of social conflict; to be more precise: of social conflict as an externalization of cerebral conflicts: "We despise primitive cultures for the taboos with which they surround sacred groves and caves and the like; but we still encourage exactly similar taboos in the antique landscapes of the mind" (6/65); To step through the mirror is to cross the meridian of an asymmetrical mind and confront temporalities which coil and veer with an alien handedness.

We can see how Fowles's fiction has changed and yet remained consistent from *The Collector* (1963) to *Mantissa* (1982): the walls of Clegg's cellar correspond to the equally imprisoning walls of Dr. Delfie's hospital room. As Fowles conceives Green and Erato as a series of masks or postures related to a conglomeration of selves, the novelist's attempts to escape become just about as frustratingly futile as Miranda's desperate efforts to get away from Clegg. In a number of ways *Mantissa* is nothing but a new *Collector:* interiorized, refined, but essentially identical—only here the artist has grasped what was previously seen as a social conflict with psychological undertones as a neurophysiological conflict with social undertones: the barriers of class have become those of the mind, the barricades of looking-glass temporalities.

There is a considerable amount of external estrangement in the Fowles novel, yet this is essentially an externalization of an internal alienation that we all sometimes sense: "I am made constantly aware of the otherness of things. They are all in some sense my counterpoles" (*The Aristos* 6/7); "All parts of my body are objects external to me: my hands, my tongue, my digestive mechanism" (6/8); "The anxiety of otherness. All is other to me, including most of myself" (2/57; see also foreword). Each cognitive repertoire is the otherness of its partner. This otherness can be divine or diabolical. In Sartre's *La Nausée* or Dickens's *Martin Chuzzlewit* the protagonist swoons in a negative transcendence while facing the utter otherness of the inanimate, whether in the meaningless singularity of a tree trunk or in the grotesque manifold of twisted chimneys glimpsed from a roof in the city. For Fowles, however, this otherness is often a rapturous transport into the new:

The ubiquitous absence of "God" in ordinary life is this sense of non-existing, of mystery, of incalculable potentiality; this eternal doubt that hovers between the thing in itself and our perception of it; this dimension in and by which all other dimensions exist. The white paper that contains a drawing; the space that contains a building; the silence that contains a sonata; the passage of time that prevents a sensation or object continuing for ever; all these are "God." (1/72)

Yet in Fowles otherness can be something very different from the potential of creativity. The alien self creates an estrangement within consciousness. The resulting difference is amnesia, expressing and denying itself in *Mantissa* as the entropy of discourse: the incestuous marriage of totalitarian narrator and blank page.

Through their imagistic encoding rather than through their scientific authenticity the various paradigms of criticism initiate a creative-associative rereading of the self as do the appearances of Juggler, Fool, Empress, Hanged Man, and Hermit in a set of Tarot cards. The games and myths of criticism are indeed no less fantastic than those of literature itself. Today *abîme*. Tomorrow cucumber. The novel is an image of an imprisoning hierarchy of meanings according to structuralist theory. Yet it is also something more than this. Criticism never quite redeems the otherness of the novel, never totally recuperates meaning: there are always leftovers, mounds of asymmetrical fallout to be lamented as "thematic emptiness," "residue," "excess," etc. It is this otherness that charges the batteries of discourse, that inoculates the text and safeguards the writer against the attacks of reification:

> So perhaps I am writing a transposed autobiography; perhaps I now live in one of the houses I have brought into the fiction; perhaps Charles is myself disguised. Perhaps it is only a game. Modern women like Sarah exist, and I have never understood them. Or perhaps I am trying to pass off a concealed book of essays on you. Instead of chapter headings, perhaps I should have written "On the Horizontality of Existence," "The Illusions of Progress," "The History of the Novel Form," "The Aetiology of Freedom," "Some Forgotten Aspects of the Victorian Age" . . . what you will. (13)

In the beacon of this *perhaps* the otherness of John Fowles may well increase rather than diminish in the course of the eleven chapters ahead of us. The Coriolis deflection of consciousness is reflected in the spiral arms of the nebulae of discourse: from the symmetry of *The Collector* Fowles's fiction drifts over the asymmetry of the *French Lieutenant's Woman* into the different symmetry of *Mantissa*. The blackhole of the text becomes the white whole of the nontext.

If the two cognitive repertoires create in divorce an otherness that expresses the irresolvable conflicts of the mind, they also occasionally meet in a violent and passionate embrace that would seem to hurl the soul of man way beyond the outer limits of the astronomical universe. In what I shall call the "orgasms" of consciousness (not necessarily those of the reading experience—except for the most sedentary) the dextral seduces the sinistral so as to assert its holism, its craving for eternity. In the final three lines of this passage from *The Magus* we witness the copulation of hemispheres, the complete interpenetration of cerebral selves:

> I was watching the star and the star was watching me. We were poised, exactly equal weights, if one can think of awareness as a weight, held level in a balance . . . and now it was millions, trillions of such consciousnesses of being, countless nuclei of hope suspended in a vast solution of hazard, a pouring out not of photons, but nöons, consciousness-of-being particles. An enormous and vertiginous sense of the innumerability . . . in which transience and unchangingness seemed integral, essential and uncontradictory. I felt like a germ that had landed, like the first penicillin microbe, not only in a culture where it was totally at home, totally nourished; but in a situation in which it was infinitely significant. A condition of acute physical and intellectual pleasure, a floating suspension, a being perfectly adjusted and *related;* a quintessential arrival. An intercognition.
>
> At the same time a parabola, a fall, an ejaculation; but the transience, the passage, had become an integral part of the knowledge of the experience. The becoming and the being were one. (36)

In St. Augustine's famous statement (see epigraph) about confronting the enigma of time the most interesting thing seems to me to be the manner in which the switch from understanding to nonunderstanding is triggered by the effort to verbalize. The world's two outstanding tennis players in recent years (a left-hander and a right-hander) achieve peak manipulospatial performance through diametrically opposite verbal strategies (verbal explosiveness and verbal deprivation),[9] and in the Augustinian dilemma I think it will be found that the major difficulty is not that of putting into words what cannot be put into words but of avoiding a transition to a different cognitive repertoire initiated by verbalization.[10] In his foreword John Fowles talks about the difference between the voiced and the mute word, and an interesting feature of the Augustinian situation is that, in its social question-answer context, it requires a particular kind of primitive stimulus-response mechanism that could be transcended only in the silent verbalization of metaphysical discourse.

Neuropsychologists study disconnected hemispheres and then hypothesize about human experience. In a way this is like making a chemical analysis of a Gothic arch to determine the structure of a cathedral. Novels *are* cathedrals. Even if we look at them as models of cathedrals, of *a* cathedral, they come in one way or another to express transmutations of cerebral hierarchies exceeding in complexity anything that today can be clearly defined by the neuropsychologist.

I hope to be able to come, in my final chapters, to a fair appreciation of the basic structure of our present cathedral, whether we call it "John Fowles," "the Fowlesian novel," "the novel," "consciousness," "discourse," "time," "temporality," "text," or "textuality": to define its blending of building materials, of decorated and perpendicular elegance, of English horizontalism and French upward-floating weightlessness. Such a conclusive overview, however, requires knowledge of a host of semi-autonomous subsystems. The architectures of these we must also examine. Whether we are within the walls and moats of the mind or of the novel we must consider the freedom of clerestory windows above the aisle roof in relation to the different freedom of rose windows giving the interior a rich and jewelled light. Before we discuss the masonry and buttressing of the facade, the slender vaulting shafts and triple arcading in the aisle of "time" as it is broken by the transept of "timelessness," we must consider the asymmetries of various minor structures, from the otherness of polygonal oriels to the queer partitions of rood-screens; from the harmony of radiating chapels to the foliated capitals of unvisited galleries. Perhaps under some forgotten canopy we can open a secret casket and in tentative whisperings articulate its mystery. We shall be disrespectfully respectful.

St. Augustine's famous statement mirrors the eternal mental

incompatibility of time felt and time understood. A key concept
in this book is that at certain critical moments the consciousness
of man turns itself inside out. I shall discuss aspects of such
qualitative changes in consciousness in the final chapters.
There I shall also try to define the temporalities of diametrically opposite modes of awareness. All such mental inversions
are caused by various dissociations of sensibility. The enormous
structural changes that take place in the mind when we fall in
love or face death are almost impossible to examine in the
clinical objectivism of the laboratory. Physicians have the same
problem with psychosomatic syndromes: one ends in a labyrinth of speculation. Nevertheless I think it is reasonable to
suggest that in the adult's existential gearing there come into
operation a number of interacting cerebral subsystems to be
strictly identified neither as those of the successive layers of
temporality deposited phylogenetically and ontogenetically in
the cerebral sediment, nor as left and right brain. We should
not think of the brain as a double tank; the cognitive styles and
repertoires take place in the entire brain just as two different
television channels coexist in potential alternation in the entire
TV-set. We may in fact think of the mind as such a television
with a sober black-and-white channel and a more vivid color
channel. We can know what channel is "on" by defining and
determing a characteristic temporality for each channel. We
may also think of such mental alternations as a series of shifts in
the sportsman's visual strategy: the aperiodic use of "split" vision which, paradoxically, creates the nonreductionism of the
panoramic approach. Charles Smithson's paleontological
"tests" may display in vertical transection the successive horizontal sediments of geological time; the mind, however, must
be sliced at all angles to become even faintly readable, and from
our literary point of view the periodizations of a simple vertical
cut disclosing the evolution of temporalities from the amoeboid
to the Einsteinian[11] will by itself be of fairly limited usefulness,
as will the purely horizontal perspective of left-right hemisphere lateralization. I will therefore be proposing a holographic model of time, fiction, and consciousness.

A well-known experiment in physics is the double-slit screen
test devised to determine the nature of light. The projection on
the wall reveals alternating bands of light and darkness as the
two slits create an interference: lightwaves overlap and cancel
one another in a patterned interplay of diffraction. I see the

alternating bands of "time" and "timelessness" in fiction precisely as such a projection from the light source of consciousness through the two slits of the hemispheres. Therefore you cannot say that the left brain "contains" time and that the right brain "contains" timelessness. Yet you can say that the interplay of sinistral and dextral channeling is somehow instrumental in weaving the enormously complex tapestry of human temporality.

Fowlesian fiction leads to neuropsychology (the cerebral world of *Mantissa*); neuropsychology leads to Fowlesian fiction. The passage below is terribly crude and primitive in comparison with *The French Lieutenant's Woman*—neuropsychologists can hardly be expected to show imaginative sophistication in impromptu fiction; yet the basic structure of internal conflict and tension is identical with that of the novel:

> Let's take an imaginary example. George is married and full of fidelity. Then a set of circumstances develops that finds George involved in an affair with another woman. George does not believe in such behavior and does not condone extramarital affairs. So, immediately after the experience, George is very much in a state of dissonance concerning his recent behavior. George initially attributes it to being drunk or being seduced. That helps, but George is soon in bed again with his new friend. As the affair continues, his dissonance increases and something must change. What usually changes is George's attitude about his marriage. Before long, he attributes his behavior to domestic tensions and comes to believe they are much worse than he had previously thought. As a result, George shortly finds himself in divorce court. . . . Why can't dissonance be a viable and chronic state for the biological organism? . . . The behavior was clearly contrary to his existing (verbally stored) belief about such matters, and normally the verbal system can exert self-control. The reason we propose is that yet another information system with a different reference and a different set of values existed in George, but because it was encoded in a particular way, its existence was not known to George's verbal system and therefore was outside of his control. (*The Integrated Mind*, pp. 155–56)

Temporality is a master-key to Fowles's fiction. *The Aristos* is not. As a nonfictional work it does not inhabit the level of holistic integration at which the structure of Fowlesian discourse is crystallized. If we look, nevertheless, at *The Aristos,* we find in the section called "The Tensional Nature of Human Reality" a subsection entitled "The Manipulation of the Tensions" which suggests that Fowles is at an early stage aware of the tension between tension and nontension in life and fiction. The qualitative changes that we see in "George" are precisely the subject of this present study of human awareness; the "affair" above, however, lacks human depth and cannot possibly function as a satisfying model for the radical revolutions that take place within the plasticity of the mind. The Fowlesian novel can. The trained reader of fiction or self knows that the cataclysms of the mind following an existential crisis are far more complex than those suggested above. I shall try to show that the key tension is not verbal/nonverbal. "George" might just as well have had a foggy, mute marriage, a sluggish, semiconscious repertoire of comfy existential gesturing which suddenly exploded into a passionate and intelligent awakening expressing itself almost daily in letters or poems or structured conversation. The crucial dichotomy is tension itself: the individual's attempts to minimize or maximize the amount of tension in his existence. I shall also try to demonstrate the way in which the human sense of time and transcendence of temporality-thresholds accurately mirrors the qualitative changes of consciousness in the adult. The cognitive style we label sinistral or Western is a subsystem. Subsystems do not have to be spatially smaller than the whole, confined to a smaller segment of the brain. Laputa is not Lilliput. The cerebral subsystem of sinistral causality is limited not because of its restriction in size or space, but because of its dwarfed relevance in the context of the whole. There is nothing healthy, balanced, symmetrical, integrated, or self-consistent in the "normal" consciousness of the adult. The trace made by the consciousness of man (history) suggests nothing consistent, nothing convincingly "sane."

The Fowlesian preoccupation with incompatible systems and the recurring patterns of specialized substrates manifests itself in the ambilateral structures of *The Collector* and *Mantissa,* the antithetical discontinuity of *The Magus* and *The French Lieutenant's Woman,* and the cross-model holographic organization of *Daniel Martin.* In *The Aristos* we encounter not only the profoundly unsatisfying Few/Many dichotomy but also other transindividual and interpersonal dualisms. The scientist's reductionism is made to face antagonistically the artist's holism:

A good scientist cuts the umbilical cord between his private personality, his emotions, his self, and his creation; his discovery of a new law, or phenomenon, or property. But a good artefact is always a limb, a branch, a second self. Science disembodies; art embodies. (9/42)

Fowles intensely resents the idea that science can digest art and incorporate the richness of artistic creativity within itself:

It is tempting to treat artefacts as phenomena that can be best apprehended when scientifically analysed and classified; thence the sciences of art history and of criticism. From this springs the illusion that all art is contained within the science that can describe, appraise and categorize it; thence, the ridiculous belief that art is finally "inferior" to science, as if nature is inferior to natural history. (9/43)
Of course I do not wish to deny the utility of a scientific criticism, a natural history, of art. But I should like to see destroyed the notion that art is a pseudo-science; that it is sufficient to *know* art; that art is knowable in the sense that an electronic circuit or a rabbit's foetus is knowable. (9/45)

In our century science has discovered general physical laws of the universe—those of relativity and quantum theory. The old Newtonian laws applied to nearly all medium-sized phenomena, to nearly everything that appeared on a human scale. But once this scale was transcended upward into the galactic or downward into the subatomic it was discovered that the laws of Newtonian physics lost their universal validity. The novelist's preoccupation with the transcendental and descendental extremes of consciousness and time may well reflect an intuitive sense of the importance of moving beyond the middle range of experience in the quest for the universal laws of the human mind.

Humanity is currently facing a global crisis of unprecedented magnitude. The period is one of swift, uncontrolled, and malignant growth: population, crime, cancer, armament, and so forth. The dispersion of our time expresses itself in the growth of cancer and missiles, but also in the endless destructive expansionism of the processes themselves. Tumors and nuclear fissions are promises of a fragmentation of life itself: "All I love and know may be burnt to ashes in one small hour:

London, New York, Paris, Athens gone in less time than it takes to count ten" (*The Aristos* 2/28).

The fragmentation of reality through technological science is the fragmentation of time through technological science. This is mirrored in a transition from dial-type to digital-type wrist-watches. What seems like an innocent piece of progress reflects a profound change of planetary consciousness, an almost imperceptible surrender to a disjointed, inorganic, and mechanical cosmology. In the dissolution of identity, in postindustrial alienation, and in the astronomers' Big Bang, the contemporary sense of a fragmentation of reality expresses itself simultaneously on a psychological, social, and cosmic level.

From the perspective of a certain brand of scientific inquiry, the distinction made at the end of this book (and in Fowles's novels) between descendental and transcendental timelessness may seem invalid. It is possible to see our state of tension within the harassing conflicts of practical life as the supreme manifestation of ontogenetic and phylogenetic complexity. All transcendence, contemplation, and ecstasy can then be dismissed as consolatory returns to a timeless and tensionless womb. Yet such scientific allocations lose all meaning and relevance within a larger framework, for man arranges his hierarchy of temporalities according to the *values* he attaches to the various levels of experience. Digital watches mark a richer, more sophisticated level of technical achievement, but also a crude impoverishment of the quality of existence. Our ultra-technological world is one of temporal Podsnappery: "of getting up at eight, shaving close at a quarter past, breakfasting at nine, going to the City at ten, coming home at half-past five, and dining at seven." The poet's or mystic's rapture in the primeval magnetism of the atemporal and nonhuman takes place beyond and above this, for having once mastered himself and time man can afford to step back, like the dwarfed people in a Romantic painting, to enrich his vision beyond the human and temporal.

In *The Aristos* John Fowles rejects an aestheticism that views the work created as a self-sufficient unit, the truths of which are internal truths, the coherence of which is a merely internal coherence. In chapter ten, "The Importance of Art," there is first a section called "Time and Art" in which he discusses "the timelessness of the artefact" and "our eagerness to conquer time." Art is "the attempt to transcend time," and he laments the emergence of style as the principal gauge of artistic worth. Content has never seemed less important; and we may see the history of the arts since the Renaissance (the last period in which content was at least conceded equal status) as the slow but now almost total triumph of the means of expression over the thing expressed (10/29).

The style/content dualism has a somewhat anachronistic ring in the poststructuralist era, yet this should not prevent us from appreciating that the desire to transcend a purely aesthetic dimension of creativity reflects a need to defy a world of windowless monads. The modern novelist's preoccupation with time is not a question of technical experimentation for its own sake. The reconstruction of the private past and the quest for a glimpse of a unified world—a vision, however inadequate, of a rounded totality—acquire a social and ideological dimension when the personal sense of an atomized experience and splintered identity is seen in the light of a fragmentation of time in modern technological society. Art may of course passively reflect anarchy and ape discontinuity, so that the novel becomes time's latest random mutation and freak addition to chaos; the critic may wish to hold that novelists merely play games with time for fun, that literature has no end beyond itself. *Mantissa* (1982) is Fowles's most elaborate comment on this theory. The imaginative work of lasting satisfaction exists as a defiance and refutation of such an ideology, and its temporal structures are devised for much more disturbing and profound aims than those of creating formal patterns and ingenious internal rhythms.

The bifurcations of *The French Lieutenant's Woman,* the excess of *The Magus,* and the discontinuity of *Daniel Martin,* suggest a postmodernist wish to eat the cake and have it rather than an antimodernist rejection of autonomy in favor of mimesis. The sober man of letters may wish to persuade us gently with his empirical mentality and English common sense, but the magus will want to go on teasing us to the limit: we must accept *and* question the nature of authorship, respect *and* disregard conventions, forget *and* remember the distinction between history and myth, time and timelessness. Cheating, breaking the rules, Fowles disregards the incompatibility of left and right. Ambidextrous, he writes simultaneously with two pens. His timelessness includes temporal sequence and his arrows of time are aimed at the atemporal. The magus is bilingual, and like his fellow islanders he has an unknown number of identities.

To be conscious is not to possess a *thing*, but to be involved in a creative activity, a changing process. Through concepts such as "mind," "thought," "time," and "consciousness" language has created an almost imperceptible reification of the being/ becoming at the heart of human existence. Without plunging into vitalism or esotericism it is perhaps possible to suspect that the mechanistic view of the universe as a machine slowly running down is a Trojan horse given to modern man by theology via post-Cartesian paradigms for scientific theory. This is a loss of *integrality*.[12] There is a splendor and fertility in life which eludes the equations of physicists, the computer cards of technocrats, and the telescopes of astronomers. We therefore do not *watch* the novelist as he maps this eldorado. In the quest for the interwoven strands of the essential life-mystery we *participate*. There are thousands upon thousands of millions of galaxies. In the fringe of one of these the ecosystem of human time is a self-generative mystery about which we really know very little—if anything at all.

2   Time Schemes

Daniel Martin starts off in 1942, in the childhood of its eponymous hero. The retrospective tone is immediately set as Dan, the mature Hollywood scriptwriter, visualizes in the form of a cinematic flashback a Devonshire tree marked by his initials and a date: the two central concepts in the novel—time and self:

> *D.H.M.*
> And underneath: *21 Aug 42.* (1)

As the story moves forward in reality it moves backward in time: chapter 13 is called "Forward Backward"; chapter 46, the last, is "Future Past." *Daniel Martin* is the story of a man moving from the film to the novel, from the New World to the Old World, from the present to the past. Through the reality of the past Dan moves from the present infernal to the present eternal; through the technical presentness of the film he manages to write a novel about the past. All is complex, contradictory, paradoxical. At first the constant manipulations with the novel's temporal dimension may seem overingenious exhibitionism from an all too insistent authorial presence. In fact, though, these temporal subtleties and ironies are perfectly adapted to the purpose of penetrating a surface reality that is in itself complex, contradictory and paradoxical.

The past of Dan's early childhood is followed by the instant now of his present life in Hollywood with Jenny, an attractive

young actress. Then a phone call from his ex-wife Nell and her
sister Jane concerning Jane's dying husband Anthony initiates a
temporal zigzag between Dan's present Hollywood existence
with Jenny and his Oxford past with Nell, Jane, and Anthony;
this temporal motion is counterpointed by a spatial movement
of an entirely different rhythm as Dan, gradually closing the
gap between California time and GMT by repeated adjust-
ments of his watch, completes the strenuous flight from Los
Angeles to London. The physical journey in time, stressed in
the resetting of clock time, mirrors on a symbolic level the
disturbing spasms of psychological time as Dan travels geo-
graphically to the Old World but also mentally to the past. In
space Dan's flight is a reality, but within reality Dan is not in
flight, in escape: he is in fact returning, and especially within
time, to a mental continent of dependence and attachment, a
temporal dimension of his life and of reality that circumstances
are forcing him with considerable pain to rediscover. The present and the past, "now" and "then," hold between them, however, a third plane in addition to those of physical and mental
reality, of clock time and psychological time; and this temporal
level is that not of Dan the traveler resetting his watch or Dan
the dreamer mentally evoking the threatening buried past, but
of Dan the film-writer arranging the sequence of events in his
past as a collage of nows in his novel "Simon Wolfe."

This is in itself quite complex: first the clock time of the
physical world where time depends on the relative positions of
traveling man and revolving planet; second the psychological
time within Dan's consciousness; and third the fictional time
within "Simon Wolfe" as it takes shape within the fictional time
of *Daniel Martin*. Yet Fowles adds further temporal dimensions.
A fourth grows out of the physical time gap between the two
continents: this is seen not only as a matter of different clock
times causing Jenny to phone Dan in the middle of the night,
but also as a matter of a cultural age difference between
America and England, and the Middle East. A fifth temporal
dimension emerges as an extension of the novel-within-a-novel
concept as we see "S WOLFE" as an anagram of "FOWLES,"
creating that mystifying Chinese-box effect of author–pseudo-
author–narrator–character which Fowles delights to toy with,
alternately marking and blurring the distinctions between each
step of a gradual progression. A sixth and final temporal dimension is added by the delicate way in which Fowles is sug-

gesting, as we shall see more clearly later, that "Simon Wolfe" throughout *Daniel Martin* is simultaneously a book about to be written in the future, a book being written in the present taking shape in perfect synchronization with *Daniel Martin,* and a book already written in the past, the last sentence of "Simon Wolfe"—"Whole sight; or all the rest is desolation"—becoming the first sentence of *Daniel Martin,* as Fowles suggests in the last sentence of *Daniel Martin.* The circle is complete. The serpent bites its own tail, as in so many mythic representations of the present eternal. The novel ends where it begins and begins where it ends, as does the first part of *Mantissa.* Thus there comes a point in the critical understanding of *Daniel Martin* where these superimposed temporal and fictional layers coalesce, beginning with the moment of Simon Wolfe's transformation into *Daniel Martin,* which automatically extends as a transformation of Daniel Martin into John Fowles. The final outcome is a work of art in which the unreality of dimensional fragmentation is so strongly felt that we accept the creator's own conception of "an eternity of presents" (19). The novel (*Daniel Martin*/"Simon Wolfe") exists as proof of the artist's (John Fowles's/Daniel Martin's) successful conquest of time.

The various stages of Dan's intercontinental flight and train trip from London to Oxford correspond to the stages of a mental reliving of suppressed memories, a psychological adjustment to abandoned emotional ties. When Jane meets him at the station in Oxford his physical and mental journeys end and meet—the converging lines of space and time intersect, and at this crucial point of merging dimensions stands Jane, who now emerges for Dan as the personification of the past itself, the embodiment of all he has chosen to suppress. Oxford becomes now. The past becomes present, comes alive in the unchanged features in Jane's face, the silent looks and mute expressions that defeat time.

The chronological looping in *Daniel Martin* is further complicated by the letters that Jenny sends from Hollywood as "contributions" to the novel that Dan hopes to write after completing the Kitchener film script. Here yet another tension is created: counterbalancing Dan's gradual reacquaintance with his English past, the eternal present of his Englishness, there is now a pull in the other direction as Jenny writes letters and makes calls from America.

Jenny's first "contribution" appears as the fourth chapter, "An Unbiased View." It appears just before Dan's sudden departure from Hollywood, whereas her next literary effort— chapter 21, "A Second Contribution"—immediately follows Dan's arrival in Oxford. This is pretty straightforward. But now Fowles begins to make a distinction in these contributions between the time of their composition in America, the time of their arrival by post in England, and the time of their appearance within the temporal multiplicity of the novel. When Dan mentions the arrival of the first contribution in the middle of chapter 26, the reader has already become familiar with it and with its predecessor in chapters 4 and 21. Chapter 34 is called "A Third Contribution." Here Fowles has allowed the gap between chronological order and presentational order, between Dan's and the reader's reading of Jenny's letter, to vanish, Dan beginning the next chapter by saying, "That little document from a different world had come by the Saturday morning post" (35). In fact, however, the reader has been informed about this third contribution more than one hundred pages earlier in a passage describing Dan's and Jenny's visit to Tsankawi, New Mexico, the site of an extinct Indian culture with its own peculiar sense of an eternal now. One notices the temporal subtleties and ironies that give *Daniel Martin* its complex and somewhat awkward impact:

> We drove east back down to Santa Fe in the splendid evening air, all roses and ochers and greens, with the tree-covered folds in the mountains behind the town lying like a gigantic crumpled velvet rug; a limpid and cloudless winter sky above, a light no camera has ever captured, or ever will, since its essence is in its depths, not its colors or vertical planes. . . .
> All of which Jenny was to describe from her own point of view, since those two snatched days were the basis of her last "contribution," whose real arrival was to come later; whose writing I now recast (but as she granted I might, at the beginning); and whose drift was why, despite her third and still-to-be-inserted contribution, she would not "give me up." In Los Angeles, she was to write, we were always "in brackets"; and for a few hours, in New Mexico, our one escape, outside them. (28)

Here the motif of contrasting media is sustained in the

references to "camera" and "brackets," the latter being both a formal reality within the passage and a metaphor from the world of writing *about* the writing of this novel: Fowles's writing of *Daniel Martin* and Daniel Martin's writing of "Simon Wolfe."

At first *Daniel Martin* seems to discuss a number of independent issues: the quest for selfhood, the understanding of freedom, the nature of Englishness, the purpose of art, and so forth. On closer examination the dualistic motifs of opposed cultures, opposed media, and opposed ideologies prove to be intimately related to each other *through time* and at the same time to be individually related *to time*. The metaphysical tetrad of the past retrospective, the present progressive, the present eternal, and the future inceptive, becomes an effective temporal paradigm for a comprehensive artistic vision defying the linearity of past-present-future. The new mirage curvatures of space-time and fiction-reality do not suggest a retrocausality in which the stream of discrete units of time is reversed; they compute, rather, a stable superspace and hypertime in which the sequential maya of glossy technocratic time gives way to a confluence of temporalities suggesting that the moment only has meaning in relation to its frame of reference. We encounter a set of parallel dualisms which interpenetrate to form the complex fabric of the novel. As human experience is filtered through the code sequences of this new conceptual suspension we glimpse various tensions: the present progressive of the film versus the present eternal of the novel; the temporal escape of America into a fictive future versus the temporal escape of England into a fictive past; Dan's consciousness of self through contemplation of the past versus Jane's consciousness of society through contemplation of the future.

For Dan the incipient novelist, this crystallization of temporal awareness takes place in New Mexico. The novel is suddenly glimpsed as the only medium that will enable him to come to terms with a cultural insufficiency removing him from an authentic experience of life: both the novel and his culture are based on a flight from the now, from the immediate flux of present reality.[13] Like the novelist, the archetypal Englishman lives at one remove from existence in the unreality of the past/future. Therefore, ironically, the only direct and "honest" way of facing this unreality must be in itself unreal. Only the unreality of the novel can capture the real world of Dan's unreality—the novel must be about a novelist:

We are above all the race that live in flashback, in the past and future; and by a long blindness I had got myself into the one artistic profession where this essence of Englishness, this psychological and emotional equivalent of the flashback (or flash-forward, flash-aside) lay completely across the natural grain of the medium—which was a constant flowing through nowness, was chained to the present image. . . .

The tiny first seed of what this book is trying to be dropped into my mind that day: a longing for a medium that would tally better with the real structure of my racial being and mind . . . something dense, interweaving, treating time as horizontal, like a skyline; not cramped, linear and progressive. It was a longing accented by something I knew of the men who had once lived at Tsankawi; of their inability to think of time except in the present, of the past and future except in terms of the present-not-here, thereby creating a kind of equivalency of memories and feelings, a totality of consciousness that fragmented modern man has completely lost. (28)[14]

What Wyndham Lewis once derided in his attacks on the Bergsonian concept of pure duration as an ecstatic fishing for the whole based on the complete interpenetration of all parts of the past is simply a very sane psychological and ethical reaction against socio-temporal atomicity. This has been formulated succinctly by Hans Meyerhoff, who distinguishes between a mechanistic pseudo-variant of this reaction based on *quantitative* escapism (Dan's Hollywood *now*, epitomized by his sterile cinematic output) and a genuine achievement of a timeless copresence of temporal elements (Dan's Tsankawi *now*, epitomized by his novel):

The more the experiential structure of time is scattered into meaningless fragments of the present, the greater the threat to the status of the self composed of these fragments, and the more demanding the quest for ransoming those *qualities* of time in terms of which the human situation (or the individual life) might be reconstructed according to a coherent, intelligible, and significant pattern.

In this sense, the literary treatment of time may itself have human or philosophical significance.[15] Despite the enormous knowledge we have accumulated about the past, the temporal perspective in the lives of individuals has become so foreshortened in our age as to condemn them to live in a perpetual present—not the experiential, qualitative co-

presence of all the elements constituting their own past re-
captured by memory, but the quantitative units of the
present as defined by the consumption of goods, news, and
the instrumental use of human beings themselves.[16]

Tsankawi is for Dan different from all other places: "in them
there was a sadness, the vanished past, the cultural loss; but
Tsankawi defeated time, all deaths. Its deserted silence was like
a sustained high note, unconquerable" (28). In this place that
defeats time Dan grasps the idea of himself conquering time, in
life and in art. As novelist he realizes the appropriateness of
using the flashback to capture an eternal present, an "equivalency of memories and feelings." As character he is then flashed
back from New Mexico to Devon and from middle age to childhood by the raven, "a bird; a voice, that always shifts me, thirty
years in the tiniest fraction of a second, to boyhood" (28). Much
later, with Jane in the equally time-saturated atmosphere of the
Pyramids, Dan experiences another such caprice of consciousness instantaneously annihilating decades of his life and bring-
ing to life Andrea, a woman he had loved in his youth:

> They stood there, alone in the shadowy room now, in si-
> lence, staring at the Isis and Osiris, brother and sister, hus-
> band and wife; for the first time since their arrival he had a
> sharp recall of Andrea, of standing here with her nearly
> twenty years before, in exactly this place, this same time of
> year—even alone like this, and for the same reason, wanting
> to savor by themselves this clear small masterpiece embedded
> in the oppressive and elephantine architecture outside. (37)

In *The Magus,* Nicholas Urfe faces such a moment of *déjà vu*
intensity as the news of Alison's suicide merges with the news
about the death of his parents:

> The first words.
> The first words.
> The whole thing had happened to me before, the same
> sensations, the same feeling that it could not be true and was
> true, of vertiginous shock and superficial calm. Coming out
> of the Randolph in Oxford with two or three other people,
> walking up to Carfax, a man under the tower selling the
> *Evening News.* Standing there, a silly girl saying "Look at
> Nicholas, he's pretending he can read." And I looked up with
> the news of the Karachi air crash and the death of my parents

in my face and said "My mother and father." As if I had just
for the first time discovered that such people existed. (51)

A further interlocking of coeternal time-fragments takes
place at the very end of *The Magus* when Nicholas suddenly
realizes that his whole life is somehow merging with that of his
mentor: he becomes aware of the uncanny way in which his
final meeting with Alison is becoming Conchis's equally dramatic and fatal meeting with Lily, in the same park, with the
same scent of lilac, but during the First World War.

Even more striking are some double exposures in *The French
Lieutenant's Woman*. Again the whole structure of the novel relies on a complicated set of temporal and situational analogies.
When Charles Smithson suddenly finds himself alone with his
newly discovered daughter, he pulls out his watch to distract
and amuse her. Here Fowles reminds the reader that Charles
had fumbled for his watch like this "once before in a similar
predicament" (60). This comment allows us first to appreciate
an extraordinary parallel that would probably have passed un-
noticed: that in the previous dandling of a watch in front of a
baby girl the mother's name was also Sarah—not Sarah his
idealized mistress, but Sarah the cockney prostitute (41).
Fowles's toying with time is of course implicitly externalized in
the ironic choice of a watch as toy. This motif of a character
playing with a watch as an ironic comment on the author-
narrator's playing with time is continued only a few pages from
the end when the author-narrator as character, an "extremely
important-looking person," stands outside Dante Gabriel Ros-
setti's residence at 16 Cheyne Walk where the two principal
characters are about to complete their final and fatal encounter:

> He is staring back towards Mr. Rossetti's house; and with an
> almost proprietory air, as if it is some new theater he has just
> bought and is pretty confident he can fill. In this he has not
> changed: he very evidently regards the world as his to possess
> and use as he likes.
>   But now he straightens. This *flânerie* in Chelsea has been a
> pleasant interlude, but more important business awaits him.
> He takes out his watch—a Breguet—and selects a small key
> from a vast number on a second gold chain. He makes a small
> adjustment to the time. It seems—though unusual in an in-
> strument from the bench of the greatest of watchmakers—

that he was running a quarter of an hour fast. It is doubly strange, for there is no visible clock by which he could have discovered the error in his own timepiece. (61)

The images of the two baby girls, the two dangling watches, and the two amorous Sarahs, serve both to connect temporally disparate events in the plot and to contrast situations that have but an ironic surface similarity—one, indeed, that frequently suggests a total reversal of circumstances.

When Charles finally meets Sarah at the end of the novel all she says is "How came you here, Mr. Smithson?" The words seem cold and laconic, but the narrator points out that Charles fails to "remember that her inquiry was identical to one he had once asked her when she came on *him* unexpectedly; but he sensed that now their positions were strangely reversed. He was now the suppliant, she the reluctant listener" (60). These motifs—reversal of power structures between characters; intrusive appearance of narrator as character—are ultimately merged in the unreality of *Mantissa*. There, behind obscuring layers of significant irrelevancy, we are offered brief glimpses of the X-ray texture of an authorial presence debased by verbalization but arrogantly defying the corrosion of literary creativity. Here, in *The French Lieutenant's Woman,* these subtle temporal cross-references give the reader vital interpretative clues and allow the pompously omniscient Victorian narrator to demonstrate his intrinsic superiority over the passive, noncreative reader. With a degree of appropriate self-mockery the author is constantly emphasizing the artificiality and unreality of the various manipulations which shape the temporal reality of the novel itself.

3   Temporal Precision

In *The French Lieutenant's Woman* we have seen the way in which
almost identical situations reach out toward each other over the
vast temporal surface of the action. The reverse would be spatially and situationally highly disparate events taking place simultaneously. This, indeed, is an equally exploited technique.
The action begins on "one incisively sharp and blustery morning in the late March of 1867." We follow Charles and his
betrothed Ernestina as they walk near the sea of Lyme Bay,
Charles with his Darwinian interest in paleontology being constantly on the outlook for fossils. In chapter 3, which begins
with a quotation from *The Origin of Species* (1859) and a brief
discussion of the Victorian attitude to time, we are still in Lyme
on this windy March day when the narrator mentions that Karl
Marx is "quietly working, as it so happened, that very afternoon
in the British Museum library." A similar establishment of exact
simultaneity occurs in chapter 19, which also, incidentally, has a
Darwinian epigraph. Here Charles has just been informally
discussing Sarah Woodruff's apparent "melancholia" with his
friend Dr. Grogan when the narrator suddenly gives us a
glimpse of Sarah while they talk about her as a neurotic female:

> At that very same moment, Sarah's bedroom lies in the
> black silence shrouding Marlborough House. She is asleep,
> turned to the right, her dark hair falling across her face and
> almost hiding it. Again you notice how peaceful, how un-
> tragic, the features are: a healthy young woman of twenty-six
> or -seven, with a slender, rounded arm thrown out, over the
> bedclothes . . . and resting over another body.

Not a man. A girl of nineteen or so, also asleep, her back to Sarah, yet very close to her, since the bed, though large, is not meant for two people.

A thought has swept into your mind; but you forget we are in the year 1867. (19)

Although these two cases are in a way quite different, since Charles has never even heard of Marx, while Sarah happens to be precisely what the two men are talking about, one cannot help noticing how in both cases the very simultaneity of the spatially separate events heightens the graphic intensity with which we visualize the characters: joining the Victorian narrator at some Olympian height, we actually see Marx bending over his books that very afternoon in London while provincial life and private emotional shifts go quietly on in Lyme Regis; we actually see Sarah's long dark hair and relaxed features as she rests naturally in peace while in another house the two conceited males pursue their learned analysis of her supposed malady. The rapid switch from one location to another within the same time-flow increases verisimilitude. The separate series of actions support each other through the confluence of time-streams, the sheer fluidity of time.

The most obvious form of temporal precision is the exact specification of clock time: Daniel Martin remembers his romantic boyhood rendezvous with sixteen-year-old Nancy as having taken place at "twenty-five past three" (30); in *The Magus* Conchis speaks of meeting his future at "four o'clock on the afternoon of April the eighteenth, 1928" (17). One would expect to find this rather trivial chronological exactitude in the more prosaic parts of the novels. In fact Fowles tends to specify clock time in fictional situations of swooning romance, cosmic transcendence. It is as if the aura of unreality surrounding these transient psychic peaks calls for the harsh counterbalancing recording of public clock time.

A further type of temporal exactness is derived from duration. Toward the end of *The Magus*, Nicholas catches a glimpse of Alison in the street below his Athens hotel room. Conchis has made him believe that Alison has committed suicide, and the brief vision of her passing beneath his window becomes utterly unreal. Here Fowles captures the temporal ambiguity of such a situation by both denying and specifying duration: "No expression, simply the stare up and across at me. No duration. It was all over in fifteen seconds" (66).

Such an exact specification of duration rounds off the climax
of *The French Lieutenant's Woman*. This is Charles's single sexual
possession of Sarah, which is not only a moment or erotic
fulfilment, but also one of social defiance and existential emancipation. The climax of the novel's action merges with the
climax of the physical act itself; the disidentified narrator
scientifically registers the ticking of the universe, the uninterrupted motion of the cosmic clockwork of reality, as in the wake
of their lovemaking these two enemies of their time abruptly
return from the transient eternity of their passion to the
infinite endurance of day-to-day existence in time:

> Her body flinched again, as it had when her foot fell from the
> stool. He conquered that instinctive constriction, and her
> arms flung round him as if she would bind him to her for
> that eternity he could not dream without her. He began to
> ejaculate at once.
> "Oh my dearest. My dearest. My sweetest angel . . . Sarah,
> Sarah . . . oh Sarah."
> A few moments later he lay still. Precisely ninety seconds
> had passed since he had left her to look into the bedroom.
> (46)

These ninety seconds seem to be qualitatively different from
the rather conventional notion of Nicholas being paralyzed for
fifteen seconds when seeing Alison in Athens or Charles standing "frozen and incredulous for five long seconds" (60) when
finding that Sarah knows about his broken engagement. Partly,
but only partly, Fowles is emphasizing a psychological truth
about our strange way of experiencing time at moments of
heightened consciousness. Yet there is on a higher level of
understanding than this a set of metaphysical implications in
the repeated preoccupation with minutes and seconds. The
whole novel is written from the point of view of a narrator
looking upon Victorian happenings with the awareness and
insight of a twentieth-century existentialism that involves a
radically different apprehension of time from that of an 1867
gentleman like Charles Smithson.

> After all, he was a Victorian. We could not expect him to see
> what we are only just beginning—and with so much more
> knowledge and the lessons of existentialist philosophy at our
> disposal—to realize ourselves: that the desire to hold and the

desire to enjoy are mutually destructive. His statement to himself should have been, "I possess this now, therefore I am happy," instead of what it so Victorianly was: "I cannot possess this forever, and therefore am sad." (10)

This existentialist conception behind *The French Lieutenant's Woman*, with its emphasis on the present moment of action and absolute freedom of choice in the now, accounts for the choice of a double ending resting not on ninety, fifteen, or five seconds, but one single second. It is the point where Charles has just accused Sarah of being an unwomanly sadist taking delight in his ruin. He is about to rush past her, open the door, and part from her forever. But there is a final moment of hesitation, a single second in which is contained all freedom and all hazard. There is no intervening power either in reality in the form of a God or in the novel in the form of a God-like narrator: for Charles and for Sarah there are two possible lines of action, just as for the reader there are two endings. The chances are exactly 50–50, the alternatives equally "real." Both possibilities must be given their fictional reality:

[*Chapter 60*]
He hesitated one last second; his face was like the poised-crumbling wall of a dam, so vast was the weight of anathema pressing to roar down. But as suddenly as she had looked guilty, he ground his jaws shut, turned on his heel and marched towards the door.
Gathering her skirt in one hand, she ran after him. . . . "I cannot let you go believing that."

[*Chapter 61*]
He hesitated one last second; his face was like the poised-crumbling walls of a dam, so vast was the weight of anathema pressing to roar down. But as suddenly as she had looked guilty, he ground his jaws shut, turned on his heel and marched towards the door.
"Mr. Smithson!". . .
"Is this not proof of what I said just now? That we had better never to have set eyes on each other again?"

In *The Magus* the protagonist and the reader must, just as in *The French Lieutenant's Woman*, choose and discriminate between mutually exclusive versions of reality. Arranging all kinds of unreal, but very realistic and credible, happenings on the island, Conchis constantly subjects Nicholas to situations in which he has to ask himself whether his experience is real or not. Nicholas is perpetually forced to define and redefine reality: to redefine *his* reality, but also, ultimately, to arrive at a metaphysical view of reality as such. The psychodrama is one in which the unit of time is completely disregarded, and in which Conchis functions simultaneously as playwright, producer, leading actor, spectator, and critic. This "metatheater" can at will carry its victim backward and forward in time. Nicholas finds himself in the unreality of Edwardian London, of Nazi-occupied Greece, and even, under hypnosis, of timelessness. It is not surprising, therefore, that in attempting to separate reality and unreality, Nicholas should turn to time itself. He checks the date of a bank remittance, of Julie's birth (in her passport) and of a newspaper cutting (46). As in a detective story time becomes the crucial factor in the careful discrimination between different versions of reality and in the final determination of one single truth, one single reality, the difference being that in Fowles's fiction the quest through time for the ultimate reality is given a much wider significance, a specific ethical purpose and metaphysical aim.

Among the forged events on the Greek island the dramatic capturing of a terrorist by men in Nazi uniforms is easily determined as unreal, as being part of Conchis's unbelievably extravagant and apparently somewhat insane drama. Nevertheless there is a certain reality behind it all, since in the real world of historical time German soldiers *had* seized Greek freedom fighters on the island during World War II. Again we are dealing only with levels of unreality, for the real historical events here are real only within the unreality of the fictional world of the novel. Fowles uses temporal precision to give the dramatic events an aura of documentary authenticity: we are given brief extracts from a German officer's reports on war crimes beginning on September 29th, 1943 at 12.45 (54).

There is mixing of fictional and historical time in *The French Lieutenant's Woman* too, but of an altogether different nature. Writing about her parents' concern for her health, Fowles remarks that Ernestina "was no more able to shift her doting parents' fixed idea than a baby to pull down a mountain. Had they but been able to see into the future! For Ernestina was to outlive all her generation. She was born in 1846. And she died on the day that Hitler invaded Poland" (5). As in *The Magus* the real time pattern of the Second World War is made to brush against the imaginary time scheme of the novel. Yet the effect is the very opposite. Here the self-satisfied assurance with which the narrator succinctly ends Ernestina's lifeline at the very point where history begins to trace the fatal time-line of a much vaster human destiny serves to stress the supreme unreality of all fiction and of all fictional characters. In *The Magus* most of the historical dates are fictive. Here they are not. Yet paradoxically, the fictive dates in *The Magus* are included for the sake of "realism," whereas the real date of the German invasion of Poland in 1939 only serves to increase the reader's sense of the story's unreality. In addition it is worth noting how the "was to" adds a certain fine touch of fate, Ernestina seeming somehow outside the control of the author, as independent of his will as the historical character of the Führer himself.

In *The French Lieutenant's Woman* temporal precision is repeatedly made to evoke a strong sense of unreality. We encounter this motif first on an ironic and naïve level as Fowles contrasts the modern view of the world's creation in some indefinite past millions of years ago with "the myth, invented by Archbishop Ussher in the seventeenth century and recorded solemnly in countless edtions of the official English Bible, that the world had been created at nine o'clock on October 26th, 4004 B.C." (19).

Sarah is known locally as "the French lieutenant's woman" because of an alleged affair with a shipwrecked Frenchman. Yet the title of the novel also refers to a French lieutenant's woman in the real world, a certain Marie Morell, who was unhappily in love with Lieutenant Emile de la Roncière, and who in regular fits of conscious hysteria forged sadistic letters that she claimed were written by the lieutenant. This forms the basis of a legal case—the unjust trial of the lieutenant in 1835 was "attended by Hugo, Balzac and George Sand among many other celebrities"—but also of a psychiatric case analyzed carefully in Dr. Karl Matthaei's *Observations Médico-psychologiques*. On the night of 24 September 1834 Marie Morell is said to have inflicted a wound on herself in order to claim that she has been assaulted by the lieutenant. The German physician explains this as hysteria: the assumption "of symptoms of disease or disability in order to gain the attention and sympathy of others: a neurosis or psychosis almost invariably caused, as we now know, by sexual repression" (28).

The whole point of this "true" story is of course that it shows striking and rather alarming resemblances to the case of Sarah Woodruff. Thus a whole new dimension is added to the novel, and from now on the reader must wonder whether Sarah is a determined woman consciously striving against the pressures of her time or merely a neurotic egotist unconscious of a suppressed sexuality driving her toward sadism and insanity.

Another dimension, and a very disturbing one, is created here by a highly unusual, weird, and daring use of temporal precision—daring, because authorial manipulation is so obvious; disturbing because a sense of fate and predestination is added to the story much in contradiction to the existentialist theme of free human action outlined in the Marxian epigraph. This counterbalancing determinism may be something we should mainly associate with Charles Smithson and the Victorians. It remains, nevertheless, a strong and insistent element in *The French Lieutenant's Woman,* and in the coinciding dates that bring the lives of Marie and Sarah together through Charles there is added a sense of unreality both artificial and haunting. There is an almost identical case in *The Magus* when Conchis suggests the existence of a supernatural link between Henrik, a Norwegian religious manic, and Alphonse de Deukans, an art-collecting count, whose vast museum of a château had gone up in flames on one single night: "I saw Henrik meet his pillar of fire at about midnight on August 17th, 1922. The fire at Givray-le-Duc began at the same hour of the same night" (45). In *The French Lieutenant's Woman* Charles gets the shock of his life when he reads about the fate of that other French lieutenant:

> He turned to the beginning of the account of the trial and soon found himself drawn fatally on into that. I need hardly say that he identified himself almost at once with the miserable Emile de La Roncière; and towards the end of the trial he came upon a date that sent a shiver down his spine. The day that other French lieutenant was condemned was the very same day that Charles had come into the world. For a moment, in that silent Dorset night, reason and science dissolved; life was a dark machine, a sinister astrology, a verdict at birth and without appeal, a zero over all.
>
> He had never felt less free. (28)

As we shall see in the next chapter, there is no real freedom for the Fowlesian protagonist without a new understanding of the past.

4 Pasts

But Owen's soul returned to him almost at once, and returned to strange
effect. He let his reins go as his lance had gone, and he even shook his
mantle away from him. But he lifted up both his hands above his head, and
. . . looking no doubt, as he felt in his coldly self-conscious brain he was
actually doing, into another dimension of life, he gasped out the words: *"The
Past is the Eternal!"*

John Cowper Powys, *Owen Glendower*

In his foreword to the revised version of *The Magus* John
Fowles claims that "all artists have to range the full extent of
their own lives freely. The rest of the world can censor and
bury their private past. We cannot." It is all a question of retaining, as Henry, the artist-magus of *The Ebony Tower* has, "an
umbilical cord to the past." In all the novels the private past of
the protagonist is intimately related to the social past of his
culture. Yet this conquest of the past takes a particular form in
each of the individual novels.

At the beginning of *Daniel Martin* the protagonist has "no
serious desire to examine my past or re-create it in any shape or
form" (7). The same goes for Anthony's wife, Jane. She is the
sister of Dan's ex-wife Nell and also that very attractive woman
who once managed to seduce Dan. When he meets her again,
though, after all those years, Jane does not make "the tiniest
reference . . . to that summer day in our past" (16). In fact Jane
seems as much in flight from the past as Dan: "I can't at the
moment take the past, Dan. In any shape or form" (18). With
Jane's daughter Rosamund, and even with his own daughter
Caroline, Dan feels he must conceal his past relationship with
Jane. A "myth of the past" must always be maintained (20).
Jane has told Caroline about this feature in Dan's personality,
but Dan has his thin excuses:

> "She said you seemed to have cut yourself from your past
> more than anyone else. Even when you were all still at uni-
> versity."

"I had a Victorian childhood, Caro. I had to get rid of it."
"Then she said you'd done the same to Oxford. When you
left."
"There's nothing very unusual about that. So do most
graduates."
"Then Mummy."
"That also happens." (24)

Exile for Dan has been temporal as well as spatial. Yet it is not
so much the remarks about his own flight from boyhood, student years and marriage that influence him. Instead it is the
oblique approach and indirect manners of his old English ac-
quaintances that make him aware of his own participation in
cultural mania for concealing reality, concealing the past. He is
quite bewildered by Jane's silences, but the climax of his frustration is reached when Nancy turns up at his Devon farm for a
short visit. Now a stout elderly woman, she fails to make the
slightest reference to their intense teenage romance. Only
afterward does Dan realize how much he is part of this temporal cowardice.

> . . . if only I had broken through the wretched plastic shell of
> that meeting, through her frightened gentility and my
> equally odious urbanity. We think we grow old, we grow wise
> and more tolerant; we just grow more lazy. I could have
> asked what happened that terrible day: what did you feel,
> how long did you go on missing me? Even if I'd only evoked a
> remembered bitterness, recrimination, it would have been
> better than that total burial, that vile, stupid and inhuman
> pretence that our pasts are not also our presents. . . . (30)

Dan is upset by Jane's emotional rigidity, her refusal to ac-
knowledge the reality of past feelings and attachments. Yet at
the same time she is a link to the past, perhaps also a key to it.
For even to keep absolute silence about the past is to admit its
power and reality. With Jane the past is always there, invisible
but present, implicit, taken for granted. With Jenny in Hollywood, though, there is no shared past, no shared temporal
origin: "Jenny's very young, Jane. With her I have to live very
much in the present. In today. The past becomes like an
infidelity . . . like a past mistress" (40).
In *The Magus* Nicholas Urfe also experiences the unreality of
the past as the unreality of Englishness. Returning from Greece

he notices a strange insularity and innocence in the British way of life. He feels "a mixture, before the English, of irritation and bafflement, of having this same language, same past, so many same things, and yet not belonging to them any more" (69). The problem, especially in *Daniel Martin,* is to be able to face the past without becoming the past. Just as the British have believed themselves to be "exempt from time" (27) on a national level, so on a personal level Anthony seems to have buried himself alive in the past: "My feeling was very strongly that he was not only living in the past, but he'd blacked out on all subsequent reality" (19).

From her neo-Marxist point of view Jane confidently dissects modern social reality with the sharp instruments of political science. Yet for Dan, who is busy discovering the complexities of locked temporal stances, this sociopolitical attitude is pseudoscientific balderdash. A psychological, or psycho-temporal, dimension is lacking in Jane's ideological anatomy, and he dryly wonders whether Marx "could have imagined a nation with only its past to live for" (31). Jane's espousal of Marxism is in itself a defiance of the past. At the same time, though, she is repeating the past: for the entire process echoes her sudden conversion to Catholicism when she married Anthony. Or is it that she is now returning even further into the past—to an unmarried, pre-Catholic self, a lost natural identity? But even this pristine past is negative for Dan. In a moment of extreme frustration over her absurdly stubborn refusal to give way to the slightest emotional spontaneity, he gives up all hope of ever reaching across the temporal chasm that eternalizes their estrangement: "He sensed that something in her was receding, not only from him, but in time, to well before his knowing of her; to an eternal unforgivingness, refusal to listen" (44).

This resembles Charles's resentful accusation of Sarah at the end of *The French Lieutenant's Woman.* Here Daniel Martin seems to have forgotten how Jane once had contrasted the healthy "existentialism" of Rabelais with contemporary English self-denial: "Always thinking about the past and worrying about the future. Never actually managing to enjoy the present" (6). Charles also revolts against a false and dangerous attitude to the past. "Charles's whole being rose up against . . . this macabre desire to go backwards into the future, mesmerized eyes on one's dead fathers instead of on one's unborn sons. It was as if his previous belief in the ghostly presence of the past had condemned him, without his ever realizing it, to a life in the grave" (48). In *The Magus,* Conchis is one more "victim of the past" (53), yet he is fully aware of the social lies that glorify the past: "Another means society employs to control hazard—to prevent a freedom of choice in its slaves—is to tell them that the past was nobler than the present" (19).

This theme of the relationship between freedom and past is strongly emphasized in *The Magus.* At the trial, Lily/Julie (as "Doctor Maxwell") argues that Nicholas's "selfishness and social inadequacy have been determined by his past, and any report which we communicate to him should make it clear that his personality deficiencies are due to circumstances outside his command" (61). She is no doubt referring to his childhood, but even quite recent deeds and misdeeds now come alive again with their full implications. Given the chance to whip the person (Lily) who has most cruelly violated his sensibility and integrity Nicholas suddenly comes to understand the inner psychological and moral meaning of the drama in which he has been forced to play simultaneously the roles of hero and fool. Whip in hand he *becomes* Wimmel, the Nazi officer:

> I tried to determine whether once again I was preconditioned not to do it, by Conchis; but I knew I had absolute freedom of choice. I could do it if I wanted.
> Then suddenly.
> I understood.
> I was not holding a cat in my hand in an underground cistern, I was in a sunlit square ten years before and in my hands I held a German sub-machine-gun. And it was not Conchis who was now playing the role of Wimmel. Wimmel was inside me, in my stiffened, backthrown arm, in all my past; above all in what I had done to Alison.
> *The better you understand freedom, the less you possess it.* (61)

Lily looks upon Nicholas's determining past as Daniel Martin looks upon his own. Depressed after failing to reach Jane, Dan sees the incompleteness of his teen-age affair with Nancy Reed as "the essential predisposing event of his emotional life . . . preforming all future relationships in his life" (43). The more Dan grows conscious of an elusive determinism in his own emotional life, the more anxious he becomes to break this sinister pattern by reaching Jane. As this becomes an increasingly vital potential step in his temporal emancipation he realizes, however, that it is made impossible by destiny, for he recognizes the same locked behavioral cycle in Jane. Beneath the surface of Jane's new political radicalism there stubbornly lives on a much more essential emotional conservatism. Dan is aware of all this, yet at the crucial moment he also sees his own cowardice, his own desire to cling to the comfortable routines and indolent habits of the past.

> He was approaching a fork,[17] the kind of situation some modern novelists met by writing both roads. For days now he had been split, internally if not outwardly, between a known past and an unknown future. That was where his disturbing feeling of not being his own master, of being a character in someone else's play, came from. The past wrote him; and hatred of change, of burning boats. (40)

As Jane and Dan travel further and further into the desolation of the desert their movement toward spatial nothingness becomes an image of emotional barrenness. It also becomes an extensive symbol of their private journey into a temporal no man's land where the past no longer counts, as well as an image of the decline of their culture into a moral and intellectual wasteland where all is becoming cheap and selfish. In the strange emptiness of a hotel dining room, and at the end of their tether, they share in the desperation of their estrangement a preposterous sense of a weird distortion of time:

> "What an extraordinary place."
> "End of the world."
> It reminds me of one of those time-warp plays."
> He gave her a quick smile. "That's exactly what I felt. When we came in. Whether we've actually really got here."
> "We're lying on the road out there somewhere." (44)

These last passages both contain references to the artist's methods of handling time (forking paths; time-warping).

What is most interesting in this travelling among temporal moods is the way in which Fowles ties up the motifs of private and social temporal dilemmas in Dan's awareness of the cultural deficiencies he shares with Jane. For him she is more than a frustrating individual. She comes to embody, partly as a

reflection of himself, a pseudo-intellectual world that conceals a
dehydration of the soul in an emotional and cultural void. The
nakedness of the landscape seems here, as the emotional tension between them moves toward some inevitable culmination,
to call for some sort of corresponding emotional frankness, a
simple straightforward authenticity that Jane in her spiritual
dearth appears unable to grant. The sexual act between them
that Dan envisages looms therefore not as a primarily erotic
fulfilment but as a sensual externalization or promise of a long
overdue metaphysical stripping:

> . . . to discover what had gone wrong, not only with Daniel
> Martin, but his generation, age, century; the unique
> selfishness of it, the futility, the ubiquitous addiction to
> wrong ends . . . not only a trip to nowhere, but an exorbitant
> fare for it. All the thoughtless effort, attachment to trivia,
> which was really a sloth—mindless energy as a substitute for
> true intelligence. Perhaps this always attacked writers
> worst. . . . He felt a more general irritation, against their
> history, *their type in time.* They took themselves, or their
> would-be moral selves, so seriously. It had indeed all been
> summed up by the mirrors in his student room: the over-
> weening narcissism of all their generation . . . all the liberal
> scruples, the concern with living right and doing right, were
> not based on external principles, but self-obsession. Perhaps
> the ultimate vulgarity lay there: in trying to conform to one's
> age's notion of spiritual nobility . . . (43–44; my italics)

There is a certain sense of hopelessness here, almost defeat-
ism—a feeling of being bereft of individual freedom, dwarfed
by the vast impersonal sweep of history. This spiritual corrosion expands as Dan bitterly visualizes an alternative past on the
occasion of a country excursion with Jane and her son much
earlier: "I rewrote history. I had married Jane, he was our son,
we had such outings all the time" (29).

When their trip on the Nile comes to an end, there comes a
moment when Jane joins Dan in this pensive retrospection, this
sadness that is at once an acceptance of the past and a retained
bitterness to what time has done. Dan's mind is arrested by a
transient lapse in Jane's self-control, a moment when her hand
had reached out for his:

> It had been in that downward look at the joined hands. . . .
> He knew it had referred mainly to the past, and not to any

specific past possibility, but all past possibility; what she knew
he knew was lost for ever; but there was also some tinge in it,
if only derived from the fact that it had been given in the
now, of a present regret . . . for what had been rediscovered,
for what, beneath all the change, had remained. (40)

The past now towers as something rigid and imprisoning that
has destroyed their chances of happiness. More immediately
the past has also suggested, in their recent experiences, possibilities that have again been missed, a certain elasticity in time
and fate that has been neglected at an enormous human cost.
Time exists not as a monolithic fact but as a plurality of dimensions, a multi-leveled hierarchy. There are, as Jane notices in
Cairo, "layers of time" (36) in reality, just as there are layers of
time in *Daniel Martin*. In the novel, in Egypt, and in the characters, these layers of time are layers of pasts—some living, some
dead; some recent, some forgotten. And in Jane, who is "dissolvent of time" (33), and for whom he feels "a kind of dry ten-
derness of time" (31), Dan sees all these pasts fused in
simultaneity, "an interweaving of strands . . . an obscure amal-
gam of rain, landscapes, pasts, fertilities, femalenesses" (33).
Visiting Anthony in hospital Dan had noticed that something
very peculiar had happened to his friend's "sense of time" (17).
Yet Dan learns something far more important from Anthony
about time than to avoid identification with the past. When
Anthony commits suicide following their brief reunion, Dan is
forced to consider the various cryptic reverberations of latent
meanings and existential hints that Anthony may have intended to suggest in the wake of this sudden and violent deed.
When Caroline asks Dan why Anthony had killed himself Dan
considers that he may have been advocating a new kind of
honesty toward the past.

> "He was a teacher all his life, Caro. I think it was a kind of
> lesson."
> "Who to?"
> "Perhaps to all of us. On taking responsibility for your
> past."
> "What responsibility?"
> "For having hated, lied, deceived. When we could all have
> tried to understand a little better."
> "But why did he wait till you were there?"
> "Perhaps because he knew I needed it more than most."
> (35)

Daniel Martin thus becomes the story of a man who studies the past to understand himself and studies himself to understand the past. The principal symbol for this preoccupation with the past is the Egyptian pyramid, with its implicit ambiguity as both a living work of art looking backward to a golden past and a place of the dead looking forward in a vain effort to eternalize the transient. The pyramid is the ultimate celebration of self-preoccupation, yet it is also something more. The East German Egyptologist that Dan and Jane meet is aware of the absurdity of devoting a lifetime to the study of the past. At the same time he knows that only an understanding of the past can give meaning and life to the present (39). The past is a tomb, but it is a tomb that can be very profitably plundered. The existentialist notion of "using the past to build the present" (40) becomes the modern equivalent of the ancient Egyptian *qadim* (39): to hold power from the past.

In the next chapter we see how the emancipated individual uses this power to select the colors of his future.

5   Evolution

The human umbilical cord, a magnificent triple-helix of two veins and one artery, invariably coils counter-clockwise.
                    Martin Gardner, *The Ambidextrous Universe*

Beneath the Pyramids, Daniel Martin comes to see an affinity between himself and those Pharaohs who also were so preoccupied with time and self: "He felt the dead around him: the ancient and their own dead, Anthony and Andrea; but richly, poetically, in the late afternoon sunlight. It occurred to him that he was perhaps not so removed from these ancient kings and queens as he liked to think" (37). With her political awareness, however, Jane finds an altogether different analogy with ancient Egypt: the Pharaohs belong to the "lucky few," the economic elite that has been living in luxury at the expense of those lower castes who have "for five thousand years . . . been given nothing, ignored, exploited" (37). Throughout the novel Dan and Jane tease and hurt each other in a continuing political argument that is only to a certain point an intellectual sublimation of their suppressed erotic aggressiveness. Not surprisingly, this ideological warfare is, like the question of their diverging attitudes to the emotional self, a matter of conflicting attitudes to time. Just before Jane's reference to the Egyptian status quo Dan makes a comment on vulgar and simple-minded Western notions of freedom. He is surprised to find himself suddenly on her side:

> "All the sales talk about total freedom being the greatest human good. Even though it's as clear as the stars up there that for the last hundred years total freedom has meant the freedom to exploit. The survival of the sharpest at making a quick buck . . ." he took a breath, then looked at her. "And this is absurd. You're making me carry coals to Newcastle." (37)

Yes, indeed. For although Dan is far more skeptical than
Jane toward any ideological system, any rigid body of political
or religious dogma, he recognizes the general truthfulness
of Jane's criticism of contemporary Western culture. The
thoughts of Antonio Gramsci he digests with surprised pleasure and interest. In fact just as Jane's day-to-day experience of
reality suggests that Dan is more or less right about the emotional decadence of their time on a private level Dan's day-to-
day experience of reality suggests that Jane is more or less right
about the cultural decadence of their time on a social level.
They are both in the temporal limbo of that existential chrysalis
(private as well as social) described by Gramsci in the epigraph:

> *The crisis consists precisely in the fact*
> *that the old is dying and the new cannot*
> *be born; in this interregnum a great*
> *variety of morbid symptoms appears.*

The achievement of *Daniel Martin* is the delineation of that
slow, complex, and unsettling process through which the socially and politically minded individual undertakes a painful
and ostensibly narcissistic inward journey in the belief that pure
personal emotions are our most profound political statements.
The novels all emphasize a basic truth: that the private cannot
be seen as distinct from the social. In each novel freedom is
achieved only through a conscious effort to comprehend and
transcend a specific social heritage. The personal and public
selves, the private and social pasts are interconnected. Man is a
social being even when striving for his independence, his individual emancipation.

In *The French Lieutenant's Woman* the individual's personal
search for an authentic private integrity and sense of true selfhood is seen throughout as something that takes place in relation to society, in the face of society, in spite of society. The
process of inner quest is to a very high degree a confrontation
with a fixed social order, a taken-for-granted set of values. In
his longing for a higher plane of existence the individual becomes increasingly aware of the extent to which his beliefs and
ideas are products of his social heritage and milieu rather than
of his own critical thinking and freedom to experience the new
and unknown. The growth of existential awareness reveals with
disturbing insistence that what has been uncritically taken for a

conscious system of values is little more than an arbitrary and unconsciously assimilated set of social habits. This Englishness that Daniel Martin, Charles Smithson, and Nicholas Urfe discover in themselves is a vague puritanism; not religious strictness and moral intolerance, but an elusive emotional indirectness. In *The French Lieutenant's Woman* the Victorian Age becomes an ideal temporal setting for a confrontation between an individual seeking freedom and a social order doing all it can to prevent this. Time here takes a specific historical form; the past becomes not so much the determining personal past, as in *Daniel Martin*, but the determining historical and social past.

The Victorian Age, however, is both past and present. In *The French Lieutenant's Woman* the now of the story precedes the now of the narration by a century. A contrast is shaped between the muddled Victorian consciousness of Charles Smithson and the detached existentialist consciousness of the modern narrator; yet at other times the author-narrator tends, like Daniel Martin, to see himself as belonging not to the avant-garde of a more advanced and emancipated culture but to the bleak infantry of post-Victorian England: "My contemporaries were all brought up in some degree of the nineteenth century, since the twentieth did not begin till 1945" (8).

Time in *The French Lieutenant's Woman*, then, is the Victorian age. But it is also time *within* the Victorian age. Fowles defines psychological time as it made itself felt a century ago:

> Though Charles liked to think of himself as a scientific young man and would probably not have been too surprised had news reached him out of the future of the airplane, the jet engine, television, radar: what *would* have astounded him was the changed attitude to time itself. The supposed great misery of our century is the lack of time . . . But for Charles, and for almost all his contemporaries and social peers, the time signature over existence was firmly *adagio*. The problem was not fitting in all that one wanted to do, but spinning out what one did to occupy the vast colonnades of leisure available. (3)

Without the passing reference to "social peers," all the talk about "vast colonnades of leisure" would of course be utter nonsense and quite incompatible with the description in the following chapter of the temporal inferno in Mrs. Poulteney's

archetypal Victorian household, where "you are expected to
rise at six, to work from half past six to eleven, to work again
from half past eleven to half past four, and then again from five
to ten, *and* every day, thus a hundred-hour week" (4). These
mutually exclusive psycho-temporal realities focus the sustained preoccupation in the novel with a model of Victorian
England as a class structure where different sections of the
community achieve successive emancipation.

From the point of view of time in the novel this means two
things. First it implies a view of social evolution where abrupt
qualitative transitions between distinctly antagonistic forms of
social structure characterize a ceaseless battle for supremacy.
Different groups aspire in turn, at certain critical moments in
history, to become dominant, to make their ethos the standard
for the whole community. Second, this approach implies a dynamic view of history as evolution, and therefore a dynamic
view of time itself. This is important, for it now becomes rather
futile to discuss the human condition. There is no such thing.
There are only human condition*s*. This struggle for supremacy
between social classes is linked in the novel to the Darwinian
concept of the survival of the fittest, the universal struggle between species. Not only does this view of history as an escalating
evolution entail a dynamic view of life and of time as change
rather than permanence, freedom of choice rather than prede-
termined repetition and cyclic fatalism; it also involves first a
confrontation *within* this dynamic, historical time-flux between
a social order based on a static concept of life (feudalism) and a
system based on the absolute necessity for change, evolution,
and economic growth (capitalism). Second, the modern view of
historical time involves the unsettling effect on the human consciousness of an entirely new and radically different temporal
cosmogony. The vast social reforms of the century that grow
out of class struggles are matched in the invisible world by a
single devastating temporal revolution. The French naturalist
Buffon had managed in 1778 to

> push the origin of the world back . . . some 75,000 years.
> Lyell's *Principles of Geology*, published between 1830 and
> 1833—and so coinciding very nicely with reform elsewhere—
> had hurled it back millions. . . . Genesis is a great lie; but it is
> also a great poem; and a six-thousand-year-old womb is

much warmer than one that stretches for two thousand million. (19)

While this enormous temporal adjustment is for the scientist as scientist a fresh wind blowing "through the century's stale metaphysical corridors" (19), it is for the scientist as human being infinitely anguishing. Charles the fossil-collecting scientist takes part in a rational and optimistic quest for the buried existential secrets of the past unfolding life as an endless becoming, time as an eternal now. Charles the fossil, the tiny human individual dwarfed by geological eternities, is part of an irrational and pessimistic adaptation to a human condition where life is petrification, time an eternal prison, evolution an illusion. This temporal paradox is at one point made to deny the whole theory of evolution as Charles, the observer of tiny extinct organisms caught in time, becomes himself a fossil in the timesected mosaic of a strange and eerie eternity:

. . . there entered his mind a brief image of that ancient disaster he had found recorded in the blue lias and brought back to Ernestina—the ammonites caught in some recession of water, a micro-catastrophe of ninety million years ago. In a vivid insight, a flash of black lightning, he saw that all life was parallel: that evolution was not vertical, ascending to a perfection, but horizontal. Time was the great fallacy; existence was without history, was always now, was always this being caught in the same fiendish machine. All those painted screens erected by man to shut out reality—history, religion, duty, social position, all were illusions, mere opium fantasies. (25)

Much of the metaphysical tension in *The French Lieutenant's Woman* is generated precisely out of this kind of contradiction between dynamic and static time, between the changing and eternal now. In all his novels Fowles recognizes a current in time moving against evolution so as to threaten civilization. In *The Magus* Conchis often tries to disillusion Nicholas about simplistic notions of progress. Discarding the good-old-days myth, Conchis nevertheless speaks of certain fine spiritual qualities that have become almost extinct in modern technological society. Here the Darwinian concept of ousted species is used to contradict evolutionary optimism:

You young people can lend your bodies now, play with them, give them as we could not. But remember that you have paid a price: that of a world rich in mystery and delicate emotion. It is not only species of animal that die out, but whole species of feeling. And if you are wise you will never pity the past for what it did not know, but pity yourself for what it did. (24)

In *Daniel Martin* there is also frustration with social evolution. As elsewhere in Fowles's fiction we find a basic belief in emancipation and enlightenment. But there is also a strong concern about disturbing trends that run parallel to material and scientific achievements and which seem to be undermining spiritual nobility and emotional authenticity. The temporal point of view is rather delicate here, for not only has the writer an ambiguous attitude himself to the Victorian class society, being both a part of it and apart from it, inevitably revolting against himself when rejecting his culture; in addition, it is difficult for him to determine whether the things he is reacting against ultimately spring out of the Victorian ethos or whether they are modern features standing in contradistinction to the old ideals, perhaps even growing out of the process of emancipation itself. Daniel Martin can talk about "our stupid, one-dimensional age" (45) while trying to convince Jane of how sexually suppressed their generation was. Yet at the beginning of the novel, when recalling the daring freedom of their gratuitous act in Oxford, Dan seems to look upon his own generation as an emancipated one healthily free from post-Victorian narrow-mindedness:

I remember those minutes . . . for their profound and delicious wickedness, their betrayal, their impossibility-actuality. . . . We seemed to take a step (that whole first postwar period, sated with the sound of marching, was obsessed with private step-taking) not into darkness so much as uniqueness; no one could ever have done this before, no other age could have had our emancipation, our eagerness to experiment. Perhaps it was really our first step into the twentieth century. (9)

Chiefly, however, the artificial worlds of cheap journalism and film production merge to create an atmosphere in which Dan, harboring within the depths of his soul a vast craving for some point of absolute spiritual integrity, comes to feel an overwhelming nausea for the whole social and cultural climate he lives in. When he meets his student companion Barney, now a television celebrity, the monumental triviality of the shoddy media world strikes him as the center of a general diffusion of cheap values in society. In the common "greed for the ephemeral," the rules have been fixed

> so that to criticize the glamorization of the worthless, the flagrant prostitution of true human values, the substitution of degree of exposure for degree of actual achievement, now invited an immediate accusation of elitism and pretension, of being out of touch. It infested all the morbid areas in their culture, the useless complications and profit-obsessed excesses of capitalism, the plastic constructs: tellyland, popland, movieland, Fleet Street, the academic circus . . . (23)

The really disturbing fact about the spiritual corrosion that Dan senses is that it is intellectuals like himself and Barney who now, in film and on television, spearhead the vulgarization of art and culture. Indeed it is this fear of having become second-rate and cheap that sets in motion Dan's entire process of self-study. It is only in sensing himself opposed to the massive body of middle-class values that the enlightened individual can retain his spiritual nobility. Only then can his identification with "the few" be justified as genuine concern for the truly human. Here the author-narrator is himself a part of the moral conflict, whereas in *The Collector* the intense criticism and rejection of a cheap and naïve materialism is carried out by a narrator-character (Miranda) who is mainly disidentified from uniformity. Miranda uses the same kind of verbal artillery as Daniel Martin. Yet the whole concept of a permeating cheapness is linked, not to the media establishment, but to a specific social class loosely called the "New People": drab, petit bourgeois social climbers like Clegg who have become spiritually dead in a cultural vacuum and by compensation live a life of material accumulation as nondescript economic cogs in the vast clockwork of the acquisitive society. Miranda hates "the New People, the new-class people with their cars and their money and their tellies and their stupid vulgarities and their stupid crawling imitation of the bourgeoisie . . . this awful deadweight of the fat little New People on everything. Corrupting everything. Vulgarizing everything. Raping the countryside . . . Everything mass-produced. Mass-everything" (Miranda's diary, November 7th).

The Collector is, like Sillitoe's *Loneliness of the Long-Distance Runner,* only on the surface a story about a psychologically disturbed young man. Both stories concern the problems of social, not individual, sickness; accepted, not outlawed, patterns of behavior. The individual insanity that seems to loom vaguely but dangerously in characters like Frederick Clegg, Nicholas Urfe, and Sarah Woodruff, is either the expression of sanity in face of social insanity or of the private form of such a cultural malady.

To look upon a book like *The Collector* from the point of view of the protagonist's individual peculiarities is to miss its essential meaning. In this parable it is what is typical about Clegg that is interesting, not the chance makeup of his surface idiosyncrasies. The meaning of *The Collector* is above all to be found on the social level: "if one word could sum up all that is wrong with our world, it is surely *inequality.* . . . And it seems madness that man himself should continue blindly to propagate this vicious virus in our world instead of trying to limit it. This was the deeper message in *The Collector;* and in this present book" (*The Aristos,* 1968 preface). Evolution, then, is an ambiguous concept in Fowles. There is progress; there is education, enlightenment, and social reform. At the same time, and apparently growing out of the very forces that propel this evolution, there is a negative undercurrent impeding genuine social achievement. Fowles refers to Shaw's argument in *Major Barbara* that material salvation must precede spiritual awakening. For Miranda's mentor G. P., though, the social reformers of twentieth-century Britain have somehow managed only to create a disastrous empty surface affluence: "He said, the New People are still the poor people. Theirs is the new form of poverty. The others hadn't any money and these haven't any soul" (Miranda's diary, November 7th).

Both *The Collector* and *The French Lieutenant's Woman* reflect a vision of a society where the basic emotional and moral dilemmas evolve out of, or must be seen in relation to, the class structure. Clegg belongs to a lower middle class that is rising; Charles Smithson to an aristocracy facing extinction. To imagine these figures apart from their social background is impossible. It is equally absurd to think of their social environment as something static. Charles's social world is disintegrating and slowly sinking into nothingness; Clegg's nouveau riche peers are the confident philistines confidently infiltrating all sections of the community. There are classes, obviously. But there is always movement within the social structure. Society is organic, living, and subject to change—subject, in other words, to time. It is here that the Darwinian and Marxian worlds converge in a "scientific" view of history as change, of an evolution that can only take place through conflict and struggle. Time is measurable and dynamic.

In *The French Lieutenant's Woman,* however, this dynamic sense of time is repeatedly contradicted. The notion of a static social state of being is in fact part and parcel of the new sociological and historical model itself. Not only do the quasi-feudal aristocracy and landed gentry proclaim the necessity of resistance to change and glorify the status quo; in addition, the idea of the struggle between classes suggests the romantic idea of primordial classlessness. This vision of a Golden Age colors many essential scenes in the novels. At Thorncombe Daniel Martin enjoys before sunrise "the pristine dominance of nature before man sullied the world" (43). In *The French Lieutenant's Woman* this sense of prehistoric harmony is developed first in the blissful pastoral atmosphere of an "antediluvian tradition" (12): the pagan love and midsummer dancing at Ware Commons, the place of Charles's and Sarah's secret rendezvous. This is a spatial retreat outside society, just as there is a temporal retreat outside society when Charles later mingles with the early risers of Lyme.

Again sunrise is linked to the dawn of evolution as Charles sinks into "that primeval classlessness of dawn population" (29). Nearing the almost subtropical Undercliff with its luscious vegetation, Charles finds himself enveloped in a sensuous nonhuman world of beautiful organic life. The atmosphere is mysteriously pantheistic, charged with the green energy of unspoiled life, of nature itself. Here in the "undefiled dawn sun" the tree trunks radiate their naked essence with a primitive significance that is about as far as we can possibly get from Sartrean nausea. The emerging vision is at once subtle and simple. It is certainly not an image of a world of perpetual change and violent struggle for survival.

> . . . there was something mysteriously religious about them, but of *a religion before religion;* a druid balm, a green sweetness over all . . . and such an infinity of greens, some almost black

in the further recesses of the foliage; from the most intense
emerald to the palest pomona. A fox crossed his path and
strangely for a moment stared, as if Charles was the intruder;
and then a little later, with an uncanny similarity, with the
same divine assumption of possession, a roe deer looked up
from its browsing; and stared in its small majesty before
quietly turning tail and slipping away into the thickets. There
is a painting by Pisanello in the National Gallery that catches
exactly such a moment: St. Hubert in an early Renaissance
forest, confronted by birds and beasts. The saint is shocked,
almost as if the victim of a practical joke, all his arrogance
dowsed by a sudden drench of Nature's profoundest secret:
the universal parity of existence. (29; my italics)

A static apprehension of time, a sense of the unchanging and
"timeless," does not only pertain to the natural world of primitive classlessness and the artificial world of inherited privilege
where Charles looks upon the family estate with a strong sense
of loyalty, affection, and purpose. Also there is present in the
novels, and especially in *The French Lieutenant's Woman,* a more
general sense of timelessness in human affairs. The love story
of Charles and Sarah is classical in its simple beauty and tragic
intensity, and at the other extreme the scenes of debauchery
have an agelessness of their own, "have probably changed less
in the course of history than those of any other human activity"
(39). Natural and social "timelessness" have a deceptive resem-
blance, and it has of course been the cunning policy of feudal
magnates deliberately to confuse the timelessness of nature (the
eternal recurrence of birth, love, death, the seasons) with the
alleged timelessness of a social order requiring the status quo
for its survival (the "eternal" supremacy of landowner over
serf, man over woman, age over youth). It is important to
understand this discrepancy before analyzing *The French
Lieutenant's Woman.*
   It is true that the feudal landowner and the modern capitalist
are seen as equally devoid of altruism: "One set of kind exploi-
ters went for the Pleasant Prospect; the others go for Higher
Productivity" (23). Yet this is the narrator's ironic point of view.
For Charles, who seems destined to inherit not only land but
also the ideology of his class, time in the sense of change and
adaptation to new circumstances means degeneration and de-
cay. The narrator sees the feudal world as cruel but beautiful
(the world of industry and commerce being equally cruel but
also ugly). Yet for Charles the external beauty and static

magnificence of the feudal world is the reflection of an eternally fixed order divinely implicit in nature itself. As a Darwinist he ought to be able to see himself and his milieu as subject to
time. Intellectual enlightenment is not enough, though. It will
take the emotional revolution of falling in love with Sarah and
all that she represents to liberate him, at least partly, from the
secure but false timelessness that initially he comes to associate
with his ancestral grounds:

> But it was the great immutable rural peace that was so
> delicious to reenter. The miles of spring sward, the back-
> ground of Wiltshire downland, the distant house now com-
> ing into view, cream and gray, with its huge cedars . . . the
> almost hidden stable row behind, with its little wooden tower
> and clock like a white exclamation mark between the inter-
> vening branches. It was symbolic, that stable clock; though
> nothing . . . was ever really urgent at Winsyatt, green todays
> flowed into green tomorrows, the only real hours were the
> solar hours . . . the sense of order was almost mechanical in its
> profundity, in one's feeling that it could not be disturbed,
> that it would always remain thus: benevolent and divine. (23)

Charles belongs to a social aristocracy, a specific historical
elite existing in time and doomed, by time, to extinction. In his
altruistic concern for emancipation, and through a certain
courage and selflessness in his quest for the authentic and human, he is also seen as belonging to a moral elite, an ethical
rather than an economic nobility, and one that exists timelessly
in all ages and periods. Yet even this conception of "the few" is
related to social realities. To begin with, though, the few are
seen as timeless:

> There runs through this succession of superseded forms we
> call existence a certain kind of afterlife. We can trace the
> Victorian gentleman's best qualities back to the parfit knights
> and *preux chevaliers* of the Middle Ages; and trace them for-
> ward into the modern gentleman, that breed we call scien-
> tists, since that is where the river has undoubtedly run. In
> other words, every culture, however undemocratic, or how-
> ever egalitarian, needs a kind of self-questioning, ethical élite
> . . . (38)

The Charleses of 1267, 1867, and 1967 "all rejected or reject
the notion of *possession* as the purpose of life" (38). The moral
aristocracy that Fowles visualizes exists throughout history as a

kind of timeless corps carrying forever, from generation to generation, the blueprint of civilization and ensuring progress whatever the social climate may be. This idea gives *The Aristos* its title. The few are timeless, and their struggle to overcome history is timeless. Yet they must exist in time, in history, as a specific group facing a specific social situation. The vain struggle of Charles against Mr. Freeman is the vain struggle of feudalism against capitalism. Freeman represents trade and commerce. He is *Homo economicus,* governing the universe not from a moral, human point of view, but from a narrow, strictly monetary one. His very name, ringing falsely with the dubious freedom of economic laissez-faire, gives him the status, almost, of some figure in a medieval morality play. As Charles's prospective father-in-law, he offers him partnership in a huge new store in Oxford Street. There is a certain superficial hauteur in Charles's rejection of this extremely advantageous offer; but there is also something more. Having visited the store, Charles experiences an intense nausea for the petty business world, for the whole monetary culture: an intense loathing of Freemanism itself.

> But there was one noble element in his rejection: a sense that the pursuit of money was an insufficient purpose in life. He . . . gained a queer sort of momentary self-respect in his nothingness, a sense that choosing to be nothing—to have nothing but prickles—was the last saving grace of a gentleman; his last freedom, almost. (38)

Yet to understand freedom is not to possess freedom, as Charles soon discovers. In the next chapter we face the pivotal issues of social and individual emancipation.

6 Emancipation

Thus in art the tension between individualism and the increasing complexity and catastrophes of the artist's environment, between the free following of dream and the rude blows of anarchic reality, wakes the artist from his dream and forces him in spite of himself to look at the world, not merely as an artist, but also as a man, as a citizen, as a sociologist.

Christopher Caudwell, *Studies and Further Studies in a Dying Culture.*

Charles Smithson is a gentleman, but he is also a Darwinist. This is his dilemma. Ultimately, *The French Lieutenant's Woman* is not so much the story of a man torn between the conventions of his time and the sexual attractions of an unusual woman embodying social and human emancipation. It is rather the story of a man who can choose, indeed who has to choose, between two ways of relating himself to time. The Darwinian theory of cryptic coloration, of the necessity to blend "with the unquestioned assumptions of one's age" (18) if one desires social survival, stands in contrast to the concepts of individual choice and free will as requirements for human emancipation.

Unlike Charles, Mr. Freeman is no Darwinist. Yet, ironically, it is he, and not Charles, who can reconcile the changed conception of evolution with his own personal interests and social outlook:

> "You will never get me to agree that we are all descended from monkeys. I find that notion blasphemous. But I thought much on . . . this theory of evolution. A species must change . . . ?"
>
> "In order to survive. It must adapt itself to changes in the environment."
>
> "Just so. Now that I can believe. . . . I have spent my life in a situation where if one does not—and very smartly—change oneself to meet the taste of the day, then one does not survive. One goes bankrupt. Times are changing, you know. This is a great age of progress." (37)

For Charles, however, capitalism is not progress. "The abstract idea of evolution was entrancing; but its practice seemed . . . fraught with ostentatious vulgarity" (37). Charles cannot imagine himself in Mr. Freeman's store, yet he knows that it is those who are most clever at adapting to the new conditions of the rapidly expanding economic market of trade and commerce who will survive. Indeed the market society of free economic competition appears as the very embodiment of the theory of the battle for survival. Charles knows that his class is doomed to extinction; that the future belongs to middle-class enterprise; that he now has a single chance of adapting and surviving, of taking the step from his own class into that of trade and business; that the gentleman has no future: the businessman is taking over, ruthlessly. He knows all this: abstractly, theoretically, intellectually.

Yet against this knowledge of the mind there is within his emotional being an instinctive understanding that for him as an individual, and ultimately also for the whole of mankind, "the meaning of life was not to be found in Freeman's store" (38). "Freemanism" is critically examined as a crude and cynical pursuit of private wealth. Its lack of any high sense of moral outlook is stressed in the focusing of the pseudo-ethical cloak of "Christian" altruism it wears to conceal a calculating narrow-mindedness:

> Indeed, Profit and Earnestness (in that order) might have been his motto. . . . Just as some tycoons of our own time go in for collecting art, covering excellent investment with a nice patina of philanthropy, Mr. Freeman contributed handsomely to the Society for the Propagation of Christian Knowledge and similar militant charities. His apprentices, improvers and the rest were atrociously lodged and exploited by our standards . . . (37)

The class model is retained as Charles leaves the Freeman town mansion after his interview with Mr. Freeman. We follow Charles as he leaves the luxurious home of this upper-middle-class tradesman to mingle with the proletarian crowds of obscure London back streets. He has himself no political or ideological awareness of the nature of his relationship to the human cattle of the metropolis, yet he dimly senses his alienation both from the affluent middle classes and from the less fortunate working classes.

What is interesting and remarkable here is that he vaguely experiences this invisible estrangement not really as the result of the economic privileges belonging to his station as a member of the upper classes but as the result of his belonging to a dying social species, a dying class that is about to be superseded by its competing and more vital enemies. In the crowded, bustling streets of mid-Victorian London Charles experiences his social superiority as an evolutionary inferiority. He is superior within the static framework of a "timeless" class society. But *in time,* within the relentless and impersonal flow of biological evolution and social "progress," he is inferior both to the powerful bourgeois with all his vulgarity (Freeman) and to the rising plebeian with all his impertinence (Sam Farrow, his servant). The three main classes come to be seen as belonging respectively to the past, present, and future. This is not intrinsically positive: evolution is merely the impersonal forward momentum of time itself, the cruel blind energy that ceaselessly creates change within the body of any organic whole, whether individual or social. Therefore, in a sense, the Darwinian notion of adaptation is a quite passive phenomenon. Not an activity, a conscious act, a chosen alternative; but a mere following of vast movements within a gigantic pattern of biological and social forces operating on the individual everywhere.

From this, and only this, point of view, Charles's passiveness becomes noble refusal. He chooses not to adapt. And in a metaphysical transition within the novel from a Darwinian to a social and existentialist level of understanding this biological refusal to adapt becomes a social refusal to conform, the existentialist act—an act of passive resistance to time itself:

> Charles was no early socialist. He did not feel the moral enormity of his privileged economic position, because he felt himself so far from privileged in other ways. The proof was all around him. By and large the passers and passed did not seem unhappy with their lots . . . But he *was* unhappy; alien and unhappy; he felt that the enormous apparatus . . . around himself was like the massive armor that had been the death warrant of so many ancient saurian species. His step slowed at this image of a superseded monster. He actually stopped, poor living fossil, as the brisker and fitter forms of life jostled busily before him, like pond amoebae under a microscope, along a small row of shops that he had come upon. (38)

Daniel Martin uses exactly this imagery as he realizes that a reactionary landowner discussing politics with Jane is doomed to defeat:

> In a few decades at most, her side must have their way. He would double and double, but never escape; the tail of a species, of a failure to adapt; and as we came up the steps to the gravel in front of the house I did finally see a justice in Jane's remark about being born mummified, since his failure to adapt was a result of the huge superstructure of land, house, tradition, family he had to carry; but the analogy was better made with the last of the brontosaurs, whose armor dragged them down. (27)

There is, then, in *The French Lieutenant's Woman,* a strong and unmistakable deterministic vein. The inevitable shadow of Hardy looms ironically. Yet transcending the toying with literary myth there is diffused through the whole novel a much more profound sense of the tragic: a rather dry and bitter apprehension of an individual fate that is at once universal and timeless. Certainly Charles bravely faces a particular social situation existing in time: the Victorian world itself. Observing Dr. Grogan and Aunt Tranter he cannot help feeling "nausea for his own time: its stifling propriety, its worship not only of the literal machine in transport and manufacturing but of the far more terrible machine now erecting in social convention" (19). At the same time, though, he is, as we have seen, not the feudal gentleman flinching at the vulgarities of bourgeois materialism, but the moral aristocrat nobly resisting time: rejecting the transient ideals of popular prejudice, defying the business present of profit right now. Charles is either paralyzed to the core of his being by the hopelessness of his situation or else provoked to an uplifting wave of aggressive feelings against the particular time-prison that threatens to suffocate him: "He stood for a moment against the vast pressures of his age; then felt cold, chilled to his innermost marrow by an icy rage against Mr. Freeman and Freemanism" (38).

Usually, though, Charles looks upon himself as a victim of time rather than as a bold knight fighting it. And whereas his active resistance to his environment is a dilemma of moral dimensions, his passive acceptance of his "fate" is, quite ironically, seen in the light of the Darwinian theory of evolution that he has embraced with such feelings of enlightenment. That this sense of fate is false and based on ignorance and self-pity is demonstrated from an existentialist point of view as the narrator offers us two possible lines of action for Charles. At this first bifurcation in *The French Lieutenant's Woman* Charles can either drive on home and dismiss the whole idea of Sarah and the vast vistas of possibilities and freedoms that she embodies; or else he can choose another road by telling Sam that they will spend the night in Exeter, where Sarah is staying at a hotel. To emphasize the existence of an actual situation of choice, there is at the precise moment when Sam asks Charles whether they will be staying in Exeter, a fork in the narrative. The question is put twice and followed by two entirely different lines of action pointing in opposed directions:

> [*Chapter 43*]
> "Are we stayin' the night, Mr. Charles?"
> "No. A carriage. A four-wheeler. It looks like rain."
>
> [*Chapter 45*]
> "Are we stayin' the night, sir?"
> Charles stares at him a moment, a decision still to make, and looks over his head at the overcast sky.
> "I fancy it will rain. We'll put up at the Ship."

As Charles here stands between a future that is a mere prolongation of his past and one which is far more dramatic and insecure, there is a second of hesitation within which his whole life seems compressed, just as it is later for Sarah when Charles rushes past her to the door. There also, we may recall, Fowles chooses to present both realities as fulfilled, both roads as taken.

Charles has freedom of choice. Yet this freedom exists only within an encircling unfreedom, for whichever way he turns, he is trapped. If he chooses the future that Ernestina represents, he will slowly suffocate in the stuffy world of Victorian convention and hypocrisy. If he chooses the human emancipation that Sarah embodies, his social banishment will prove as severe as her own. What he has not realized, at this point, is that even this brave choice of the difficult turning in the maze brings only further moments of anguish. The process of emancipation does not involve a single choice, a single moment of indecision and pain, but a lifetime of discomfort and struggle:

> . . . you thought . . . to prove to yourself you were not yet in the prison of your future. But escape is not one act, my

friend. . . . Each day, Charles, each hour, it has to be taken
again. Each minute the nail waits to be hammered in. You
know your choice. You stay in prison, what your time calls
duty, honor, self-respect, and you are comfortably safe. Or
you are free and crucified. Your only companions the stones,
the thorns, the turning backs; the silence of cities, and their
hate. (48)

And so we arrive at the basic questions that Fowles asks in *The
French Lieutenant's Woman*. Is there predestination or freedom?
Is life passive suffering or active emancipation?

Slowly the answers are squeezed out of a complex and enigmatic reality. There is freedom within unfreedom; there may
be emancipation if there is active suffering. The individual has
a timeless freedom of choice; yet this eternally repeated moment of choice always exists within the prison of time itself—
there is for each situation of choice only a limited set of
alternatives conditioned by the particular point of time at which
the individual happens to live. Man can choose; but he cannot
choose the situation within which he must make his choice.
Charles becomes aware of himself and of the Victorian trap—
and this consciousness is liberating; he also, however, becomes
conscious of a much vaster trap, that of the human condition
itself—and this consciousness is imprisoning.

The idea of active suffering is developed first on a superficial
level in the various hints of masochism in Sarah and others. On
a higher level of understanding this concept belongs to the
metaphysical center of *The French Lieutenant's Woman* and
reaches a beautiful apex in the image of crucifixion. For
Charles things would be simpler if he could see himself choos-
ing between actively resisting and passively continuing his
sterile mode of existence within the crippling Victorian way of
life. Knowing, however, that resistance will also imply sacrifice
and renunciation, he experiences the problem, the choice itself,
as an enemy: "it was almost palpable, not passive but active,
driving him forwards into a future it, not he, would choose"
(48). This feeling is accentuated for Charles as he feels that he
is guided along the road to freedom by Sarah. She is always a
step ahead of him, and although he often feels that she is only
the embodiment of something elusive and liberating, he eventually comes to experience so close an identification between
Sarah and his own emancipation, that both seem to vanish together when Sarah slips from his possessive hold.

If Sarah, nevertheless, on one level, seems for Charles to stand between himself and his happiness, since it is only with her that he can imagine any living future, she can on a less personal and myopic plane become for him the way to emancipation—one achieved not *with* her, but *through* her. Entering a nearby church to gain some inner peace after the shattering experience of his brief sexual possession of Sarah, Charles contemplates in a reflective, agnostic mood the figure of Christ on the cross. Gradually, he comes to see a subtler symbolism in the crucifixion than that generally offered by established religion. First, he sees himself on the cross—the victim, the passive sufferer. Then he sees himself crucified on Sarah, but this blasphemous image immediately gives way to a vision of Sarah standing there beside him actively removing him from the cross. In this achieved togetherness, so different from the conventional social interdependence that he keeps striving for, the time-determined activity of social emancipation merges, in a painfully beautiful synthesis, with the timeless passiveness of human suffering. Cosmic as this vision becomes in the widest dimensions of its significance, it leaves us with a glimpse, not of a confused young Victorian torn between the social conventions and the scientific theories of his time, but of man himself, wonderfully and gloriously free in the moment of his conscious transcendence of quotidian time, yet pitifully stranded none the less in one of the countless frozen moments of time—a helpless, insignificant organism petrified in fractions of a second into eternal silence. Here the Victorian age is at once a *specific* age and *any* age confronting the individual with its stale dogma and convention:

Rather she seemed there beside him, as it were awaiting the marriage service; yet with another end in view. For a moment he could not seize it—and then it came.

To uncrucify!

In a sudden flash of illumination Charles saw the right purpose of Christianity; it was not to celebrate this barbarous image, not to maintain it on high because there was a useful profit—the redemption of sins—to be derived from so doing, but to bring about a world in which the hanging man could be descended, could be seen not with the rictus of agony on his face, but the smiling peace of a victory brought about by, and in, living men and women.

He seemed as he stood there to see all his age . . . as the

great hidden enemy of all his deepest yearnings. That was
what had deceived him . . . the cancer, the vital flaw that had
brought him to what he was: more an indecision than a reality, more a dream than a man, more a silence than a word, a
bone than an action. And fossils!
    He had become, while still alive, as if dead. (48)

    Whether Sarah really does uncrucify Charles is very doubt-
ful. From a certain point of view she seems bent on crucifying
him. Her real aim is to uncrucify herself, and in this she becomes much more than an individual desiring personal freedom. She comes to embody the emancipation of woman. *Every
emancipation,* we read in the Marxian epigraph, *is a restoration of
the human world and of human relationships to man himself.* This
suggests the theme of woman's emancipation from man. At the
same time the statement stresses the way in which every specific
process of liberation is part of a much vaster human emancipation. This is how the apparent contradiction between the idea
of Sarah's selfish pursuit of her own freedom and the idea of
her uncrucifying Charles is resolved in the concept of women
giving men freedom by achieving their own emancipation—the
vision of a woman loving a man by refusing to allow him eternal
possession. Charles's attitude to female emancipation is highly
ambiguous. Emotionally, he often comes to look upon himself
as a victim of some timeless feminine selfishness driving woman
to subject and enslave man. In the church, after his possession
of Sarah but before his vision of uncrucifixion, Charles is torn
and split by an intense ambivalence. He is stunned by the realization that Sarah is never going to permit possession in terms
of one human being actually owning another. He resents having been seduced, having been outwitted, having "fallen into
her snare" (48). At the same time his more generous self listens
to a nobler inner voice: "perhaps there is one thing she loves
more than you. And what you do not understand is that because she truly loves you she must give you the thing she loves
more" (48). Charles's view of Sarah as a manipulating and
scheming female does not fade for ever at this point, though.
At the very end he accuses her of an "unwomanly hatred of my
sex" and sees himself as "a footsoldier, a pawn in a far vaster
battle . . . not about love, but about possession and territory"
(60). There is considerable self-pity in Charles here, but there is
also something really tragic in his being alienated both from his

own age and from the emancipated future that Sarah seems to anticipate.

Sarah seems to sense that she belongs to another age, to the future. In contrast with Ernestina, who has "exactly the right face for her age" (5), in which "the favored feminine look was the demure, the obedient, the shy" (2), Sarah has the frank countenance and direct look of the modern emancipated woman of the twentieth century, an expression that in the nineteenth century is entirely disconcerting: "We can sometimes recognize the looks of a century ago on a modern face; but never those of a century to come" (21). A parallel here is Lily in *The Magus*. Nicholas first sees her in the role of a mysteriously elusive beauty from the time of the First World War. At the end of the novel she has outwitted Nicholas, just as Sarah outwits Charles: "Lily now seemed to me as far ahead of me in time as she had at first started behind" (62).

More clearly than Charles, and without the benefit of Darwinian theory, Sarah sees their century as a temporal prison that chance has placed them in: "You have given me the consolation of believing that in another world, another age, another life, I might have been your wife. You have given me the strength to go on living . . . in the here and now" (47).

Sarah is, to a higher degree than Charles, aware of her own situation, conscious of her own struggle, of its purpose and meaning. In contrast with Charles she is able to live up to Arnold's idea of *acting what one knows* (61). Charles knows, but his position within Victorian society is so firmly cemented that each act is the outcome of painful inner struggle. This gives to his most insignificant deeds and decisions a wider meaning within the vaster framework of the individual's timeless confrontation with the human condition. The fact that Charles is continuously torn between knowledge and habit, between social consciousness and social conventions, makes him, although he lacks the haunting psychic magnetism of the mysterious heroine, a more complex and interesting figure than Sarah. Not only is Charles incapable of acting directly in accordance with the knowledge he possesses as an intelligent Darwinist and sensitive lover; in addition his knowledge is in itself only partial. To a certain extent he is aware of male chauvinism and the more obvious forms of the suppression of women in his time. Yet his attitude to Sarah frequently reveals a complete ignorance of how he is himself part of the vast apparatus of mas-

culine aggression and dominance. Here Fowles very deliberately emphasizes the historical situation. Time here is not only
an age—the typically masculine age of Victorian England with
its factories, imperialism, and aggressive expansion. Time is
also a more particular historical moment—the birth of feminism:

> But remember the date of this evening: April 6th, 1867. At
> Westminster only one week before John Stuart Mill had
> seized an opportunity in one of the early debates on the
> Reform Bill to argue that now was the time to give women
> equal rights at the ballot box. . . . March 30th, 1867, is the
> point from which we can date the beginning of feminine
> emancipation in England. . . (16)

Charles's partial awareness of the sexism of his time is more
credible than Sarah's rather implausible feminine consciousness. Although it may be intended to be seen as symbolic, her
struggle for emancipation remains very private. She is no femi-
nist and Charles is no socialist. Nor is either of them an existentialist. And yet Fowles gives their private conflicts a wider
human significance that allows us to see their struggles with
themselves and each other in relation to feminism, socialism,
and existentialism.

The battlefield is one where every victory hurts. The crusade
is, as Fowles suggests when speaking of *amour courtois* in his note
to "Eliduc" in *The Ebony Tower,* "a desperately needed attempt
to bring more civilization (more female intelligence) into a
brutal society."

7 The Eternal Now

Ces courts moments de délire et de passion, quelque vifs qu'ils puissent être, ne sont cependant, et par leur vivacité même, que des points bien clairsemés dans la ligne de la vie. Ils sont trop rares et trop rapides pour constituer un état et le bonheur que mon cœur regrette n'est point composé d'instants fugitifs mais un état simple et permanent, qui n'a rien de vif en lui-même, mais dont la durée accroît le charme au point d'y trouver enfin la suprême félicité.

J. J. Rousseau, *Les Rêveries*

Writing about his experience on the Greek island of Spetsai ("Phraxos" in *The Magus*) John Fowles stresses the feeling of timelessness:

Away from its inhabited corner Spetsai was truly haunted, though by subtler—and more beautiful—ghosts than those I have created. Its pine-forest silences were uncanny, unlike those I have experienced anywhere else; like an eternally blank page waiting for a note or a word. They gave the most curious sense of timelessness and of incipient myth. . . . The *genius loci* was very similar indeed to that of Mallarmé's finest poems of the unseen flight, of words defeated before the inexpressible. I am hard put to convey the importance of this experience for me as a writer. It imbued and marked me far more profoundly than any of my more social and physical memories of the place. I already knew I was a permanent exile from many aspects of English society, but a novelist has to enter deeper exiles still. (foreword)

In *The French Lieutenant's Woman*, the new sense of the timelessness of creation given by the geologists was by no means comforting to those accustomed to the time scheme of their biblical cosmogony. A negative view of eternity as the mere infinite extension of a line is of course primitive; the temporal infinity that Fowles usually presents us with has none of this mind-boggling anguish. Instead timelessness is a state of exalted emotional being, often suffused by a delicate sense of existential privilege, a thrill of cosmic initiation.

In *The Magus* Fowles continually connects timelessness with Greece. In fact the general kind of "timelessness" that is connected with Greece in this novel is really no timelessness at all and has little to do with the eternal now or the eternal moment. There is a *feeling* of timelessness, but this feeling is derived from the idea of ancient Greece—temporally of course quite a finite phenomenon—and from an atmosphere of unchangingness that is experienced as timeless. In addition there is a general sense of this ancient culture being timeless on account of the "timeless" truths that belong to its art and thought. On Parnassus a muleteer tells Nicholas Urfe about the shepherd life, "a life of sun-hours, counting, milking, brittle stars and chilling winds, endless silences broken only by bells, alarms against wolves and eagles; a life unchanged in the last six thousand years" (40). Time here, measured by the sun, is the biological time of nature, the cosmic time of the infinite astronomical universe, not the public clock time of a finite society: "It was the world before the machine, almost before man" (7). The restful peace, the silent solitude of the classical landscape removes Nicholas from the dynamic time of civilization to the static time of nature, from the hours, minutes, and seconds of the London rat race to the timelessness of Greece. It is true that the vast vistas of silence and solitude give Nicholas ample time to reflect upon the past; "I knew that on the island one was driven back into the past. There was so much space, so much silence, so few meetings that one too easily saw out of the present, and then the past seemed ten times closer than it was" (11). Yet these moments of retrospection are rare. Mostly time stands still on the island, just as it always has. Nicholas dozes in the shade of the pines, "in the agelessness, the absolute dissociation of wild Greece" (12).[18]

The twin actresses belong respectively to time and timelessness. Rose/June has studied modern languages and is more prosaic. She stands for time, as does Alison the stewardess who now lives in the faraway world of timetables. Lily/Julie has studied Latin and Greek. She stands for timelessness—both in the role of romantic mistress and in that of a schizophrene who has lost all sense of time. "Unlike any modern girl" (42), she embodies the mythic past, the forever removed mysteries of ancient history, human life made divine by the sheer sweep of time. Nicholas's visit to Greece, his stay on Phraxos, his walks to Bourani, and his meetings there with Conchis and Lily/Julie become an escape from quotidian time. He gains magical access to a forbidden world of timeless mystery and enchantment. Walking back from the headland of Bourani and his first mysterious meeting with Conchis, Nicholas has a strange feeling

> of having entered a myth; a knowledge of what it was like physically, *moment by moment,* to have been *young and ancient,* a Ulysses on his way to meet Circe, a Theseus on his journey to Crete, an Oedipus still searching for his destiny. I could not describe it. It was not in the least a literary feeling, but an intensely mysterious *present* and concrete feeling of excitement, of being in a situation where anything still might happen. As if the world had suddenly, during those last three days, been re-invented, and for me alone. (25; my italics)

I have stressed *present* here, for in *The Magus,* as well as in *The French Lieutenant's Woman* and *Daniel Martin,* timelessness is connected with presentness. Take, for instance, the scene where Daniel Martin contemplates Rembrandt's self-portrait:

> The sad, proud old man stared *eternally* out of his canvas, out of the entire knowledge of his own genius and of the inadequacy of genius before human reality. Dan stared back. The painting seemed uncomfortable in its *eighteenth-century* drawing-room, telling a truth such decors had been evolved to exclude. The supreme nobility of such art, the plebeian simplicity of such sadness; an immortal, a morose old Dutchman; the deepest inner loneliness, the being on trivial public show; *a date* beneath a frame, *a presentness beyond all time,* fashion, language; a puffed face, a pair of rheumy eyes, and a profound and unassuageable vision.
> Dan felt dwarfed, in *his century,* his personal being, his own art. The great picture seemed to denounce, almost to repel. Yet it lived, it was *timeless....* (46; my italics)

I have stressed, here, the way in which Fowles brings time and timelessness to work on each other, but above all the phrase "a presentness beyond all time." From a certain metaphysical point of view there is no past or future, only presentness, as Charles had sensed in *The French Lieutenant's Woman:* "Time was the great fallacy; existence was without history, was always now" (25). In *Daniel Martin* this is central. We meet it when Dan thinks of the Tsankawi Indians and "of their inability to think of time except in the present, of the past and future except in terms of the present-not-here" (28). Later, just after having sent an Egyptian postcard to Jenny describing Kitchener's Island as wonderfully *"out of time"* (41), Dan is sitting in a rather vulgar restaurant thinking of how beautiful Jane had looked for a moment:

> . . . a strange softness, a gravity, she had been looking down through the water. It would have made a lovely photograph, but the moment was too transient; though that was also its beauty. . . . He was too English, of course, to take Zen very seriously as a philosophy, but it had strengthened in him a feeling that some inner truth lay in the perception of the transient. He would have been embarrassed to define and justify it, but it lay somewhere in the importance of present-ness in life; just as the value he attached to it was betrayed by his demanding or expecting more of the present than it was usually prepared to give. This was why, for instance, he had no deep political convictions, since they must depend on some form, however attenuated, of perfectibility, of belief in future; and why he could trace his actual feeling of irritation to the experience of Philae, a present about to disappear for ever, and to this crammed horror of a restaurant, a present one wished *would* disappear for ever; while Jane was a combi-nation of both, a present about to disappear and, in her would-be socialist and independent self, a present that barred him from what little was left of the first kind. (41)

We see here how obsessed Fowles is with time. We see also how the principal motifs (Englishness, ideology, vulgarity, love, transcendence) are expressed in temporal terms and therefore given, through time, vital relationships to each other. Thus time functions as an interlocking organizing principle which brings order to what first looks like a chaotic and heteroge-neous body of random ideas. Through time, through a recog-nition and appreciation of a temporal perspective, we discern the outline of a sophisticated moral and aesthetic vision.

In *Daniel Martin* style and form are inseparable from mean-ing and content. When we see Dan, at the beginning, as he "sits with his back to a beech-trunk, staring down through foliage at the field [without] past or future, purged of tenses"(1), the boy's sense of inner peace through presentness is stressed in two ways: first in the use of the present tense; then in "purged of tenses," which suggests the present eternal within the psychological stance of Dan the character, and also the present eternal within the temporal outlook of Dan/Fowles the narrator. This narrator has traveled back into the past with such imaginative intensity that time has lost all meaning. There is only presentness. The present ceases to be a tense. It is timeless. Thus the mental effort of the artist-protagonist creates precisely that "kind of equivalency of memories and feelings," that eternal present, which once used to characterize the temporal awareness of the Tsankawi Indian, and which Dan has now transferred to the formal plane of his self-study—the layers of nows that Fowles has worked out for the time scheme.

Fowles, then, adds an extra dimension to his writing by elegant interpolation of running comments ("purged of tenses") on the process of writing itself. In *The French Lieutenant's Woman* this added dimension is provided by the intrusive narrator. In *The Magus* it is Conchis's unbelievable metatheater that serves as a kind of structural chorus allowing the artist-creator to comment through symbols and mythic happenings on the protagonist's anguished struggle with the relationship between fiction and reality. In *Daniel Martin* this fictional introspection is established through the idea of Dan the protagonist writing film scripts and Dan the inceptive novelist shaping his self-study "Simon Wolfe." Dan the script-writer who suddenly sees "a chance to use a flashback inside a flashback, and possibly a flashback inside that as well" (33), is simultaneously Dan the novelist structuring "Simon Wolfe," or, if you will, John Fowles structuring *Daniel Martin*. Coexistent with this parallel between film and fiction, there is, as we have seen, a contrast. The film stands for presentness (the eternal now of the film reel as well as of the Hollywood lifestyle), whereas the traditional novel is an expression of the past/future: "Film excludes all but now; permits no glances away to past and future" (15).

Miniature lectures on the art of writing fiction may border on the overingenious. Yet they are also part of the psychological analysis of the way in which the characters are alienated from each other through their differing attitudes to time:

A novel is written in the two past tenses: the present perfect of the writer's mind, the concluded past of fictional convention. But in terms of the cramped and myopic fictional present . . . if Jenny accuses Dan (has still, of course, in the chronology of this reconstruction, hardly put pencil to paper, let alone had Dan read the result) of a love of loss, she is being disingenuous, since . . . she knows he knows that behind her reproaches lies a very old-fashioned little nucleus of personal vanity; a myth of permanence. She will not be one of a chain, she will last. (22)

Fowles sets the present against the past/future. Dan is brought up in the past/future–minded culture of England; but he is also in revolt against this culture. He is torn between Jenny, who represents the presentness of the Now generation and Jane, who embodies the past/future and therefore becomes a frustratingly Janus-faced generator of ambivalence. In one of her contributions Jenny speaks of an affair with a young actor called Steve. This experience had shaped itself as an eternal erotic now. No past. No future. No love. "To have it without any sort of love. Just through the body. Knowing yesterday doesn't matter, tomorrow doesn't matter" (34).

This connection between sexual relationships and presentness is a characteristic phenomenon in the lives of Fowles's protagonists. It may reflect a mature existentialist acceptance of the facts of life, the laws of love; but it may also reflect immature escapism, a cynical egotism that the protagonist must consciously abandon in order to survive and transcend his individuality. *Daniel Martin* has all kinds of brief and futureless sexual affairs. Mentioning briefly his relationship with a rather vapid starlet known erotically as the "British Open," Dan reflects on the futurelessness of their lovemaking (14). In Oxford, Jane had seen no danger in this particular mixture of Time and Eros:

> "Just once. An *acte gratuit?*"
> He stared at his shoes. "And tomorrow?"
> "If we knew exactly what we were doing. That we could keep it . . . outside time." (6)

But they could not. The act haunts Dan, and it undermines their new relationship of mutual respect and understanding. Dan cannot see Jane as presentness, as pastlessness. In order to possess her mentally or physically, this man of self-centered presentness must relinquish his attitude to women, to himself, and to time. There can be no future—at least no future with Jane—if the past remains forgotten or suppressed. Therefore, when they come together again sexually in Palmyra after so many years of separation, Jane cannot retain her former belief in keeping a single sexual act "outside time." She now knows that, in love, today is threatened by the sheer inevitability of tomorrow. Love as an experience may exist in the infinite timelessness of the now. But love as a relationship must exist in time, in the organic fusion of past and future, not in the limbo between them.

In *The Magus* Nicholas Urfe's relationship with Alison had been one in which the future was something unreal: "Always we edged away from the brink of the future. We talked about *a* future, about living in a cottage, where I should write, about buying a jeep and crossing Australia. 'When we're in Alice Springs . . .' became a sort of joke—in never-never land" (4). The forced *joie de vivre* of their voluptuous but primitive domestic life takes place in a private world "as remote from ordinary time as [they] were from the dull London world outside the windows" (4). Then, when Nicholas leaves to take a teaching job in Greece, he decides to forget Alison. She simply ceases to exist. So does all the emotional past. It is indeed for this crime of spiritual and temporal perversity that Conchis later punishes and "treats" Nicholas.

On the magic island Nicholas continues his casual sexual life. He gets treated for supposed venereal contamination—an obvious symbol for his inner state of disease—but this leaves him just as unconcerned about the future as about the past: "I did not think about the future. . . . The pattern of destiny seemed clear: down and down, and down" (9). The danger of this kind of escape from the past/future into a primitive and sensual presentness is further emphasized when Lily/Julie, who is supposed to be schizophrenic, is said to have lost her sense of time. According to Conchis she "lives in the present. She does not remember her personal past—she has no past" (27). Here, in fact, Conchis is not describing Julie's mental state (she is perfectly healthy) but suggesting a basic insanity in Nicholas's attitude to life, to other people, to himself . . . to time. This analysis of Nicholas's relationship to women and time is given a strange twist toward the end of the novel in the description of

his feelings for Lily/Julie. Alison he could love only in the
present; Lily/Julie he can love only in the past: "I could have
longed for certain aspects of her, for certain phases—but it was
that very phasality that made her impossible to love. So I could
almost think of her, the light-phase her, as one thinks tenderly
but historically of the moments of poetry in one's life; and yet
still hate her for her real, her black present being" (70).

In Hollywood, Jenny feels that England lacks a future: "I
know California is the future and England is already a thing in
a museum, a dying animal in a zoo" (21). For Daniel Martin it is
not only England but the whole world that is without future.
Life is an eternal waiting for something that will never come.
He sees "existence as a waiting-room" (39), the SALLE D'AT-
TENTE of Conchis's miniature universe (10). Jenny stresses
how much the culture of Dan's private past is the past in a
wider, social sense, and how much the culture of Dan's present
is the future.

> I begin to see it as a choice of how you pay the bill. At home
> we do it by being apathetic and hierarchical, by clinging to
> the past. Here they do it by looking forward to a dream
> world, where everyone succeeds. . . . Today's problems aren't
> problems, but proofs of tomorrow's new frontier. You drive
> on, at all costs. With us, you make do with what you are.
> They're eternally stuck in the first few pages, when we
> reached the last chapter ages ago. (21)

The future, then, is America. But it is not all as simple as that
for Dan. First, as we have seen, because he is being forced to
return to England and confront his "unwritten worlds; his past
futures, his future pasts" (33). Second, because he is involved
with movies. Hollywood is part of the future-oriented culture
of America. At the same time Dan feels that the film is the
medium of the present, of the eternally flowing now. Thus
cinematic art stands, temporally, outside the continents that
Dan is torn between (England and pure pastness; America and
pure futurity), offering a form of escape from both. Gradually,
Dan comes to see this escape as a cowardly flight. The Tsankawi
experience was one of true nowness; Hollywood is a false
nowness. In *The French Lieutenant's Woman* the same discrimination is made between two opposite ways of living in the now.
First, Charles experiences a false presentness as he attempts to

dull the pain of life (and love) through an orgy of sensual stimulation, a creature present. Then, on a much higher level of reality, he acquires an authentic sense of the eternal now.

> Earlier that evening, when he was in Sir Tom's brougham, he had had a false sense of living in the present; his rejection then of his past and future had been a mere vicious plunge into irresponsible oblivion. Now he had a far more profound and genuine intuition of the great human illusion about time, which is that its reality is like that of a road—on which one can constantly see where one was and where one probably will be—instead of the truth: that time is a room, a now so close to us that we regularly fail to see it. (41)

After this moment of insight Charles feels "suddenly able to face his future" (41). Daniel Martin, on the other hand, lives in an escapist presentness that is not an understanding of time but a blindness to it: "I had no project in mind . . . I was not really flying to New York, and home; but into an empty space" (7). This sense of emptiness is intensified by an almost neurotic evasion of the past. As we have seen, though, Dan comes to a point in his personal and artistic development where he realizes that all real art and all authentic human action presuppose an understanding of the self and the will and courage to achieve such an understanding. Authentic art requires a new understanding of self, just as a radically different society requires a new understanding of language. Communication is the basis of society, and therefore the individual in revolt must turn first toward himself, toward consciousness and language, as Fowles suggests in *The Ebony Tower* through the subversive semiology of Roland Barthes's *Mythologies:*

> "there are all kinds of category of sign by which we communicate . . . one of the most suspect is language—principally for Barthes because it's been very badly corrupted and distorted by the capitalist power structure. . . . People like Barthes are more interested in making people aware of how they communicate and try to control one another. The relation between the overt signs, whether they're verbal or not, and the real meaning of what is happening."
> "But you have to change society first, don't you?"
> "One hopes that's what more awareness does." ("The Cloud")

The decision to undertake a brave, uncompromising self-study is a moment of absolute catharsis in *Daniel Martin*. The novel is the story of a man moving toward a decision to paint a self-portrait. At the same time the novel is this self-portrait—the story of a man who abandons the present progressive of film for the past/future and present eternal of the novel. It is a novel about writing a novel—or failing to write a novel.

8   The Eternal Moment

I was feelin' kinda lonesome and blue,
I needed somebody to talk to.
So I called up the operator of time
Just to hear a voice of some kind.
"When you hear the beep
It will be three o'clock."
She said that for over an hour
And I hung up.

Bob Dylan, *Talkin' World War III Blues*

Timelessness may grow out of presentness. But it may also grow out of an eerie sense of suspension, a feeling that the flow of time has been temporarily broken. You are removed, for a brief moment, to another dimension existing outside time. Time stops.

Savoring the sweetness of the Egyptian dawn Daniel Martin feels "the pristine dominance of nature before man sullied the world." This sense of primordial timelessness is experienced as a "suspension of time" (43) as Dan informs Jane that his watch has stopped. A bit later the renewed physical contact with Jane brings Dan so abruptly back to their lovemaking in Oxford that time disappears: "suddenly, in that first naked contact, . . . there was no time, no lost years, marriage, motherhood, but the original girl's body" (44). Here Dan is taken from one reality to another; from a present nakedness to a past nakedness, the two faraway but coeternal moments meeting because of their similarity. But when Nicholas loses his sense of time in *The Magus* as he is brutally taken from Lily/Julie to the Kafkaesque trial, there is no movement within time itself but simply a nebulous sense of timelessness as one level of unreality gives way to another, more disturbing one. For five days time is a blank for Nicholas. The trial removes him to a state of such incredible unreality that the word *time* becomes utterly meaningless.

In *The French Lieutenant's Woman* Ernestina's diary is temporarily discontinued at the date of her first romance with Charles. This blank within time denotes unreality too, but it is extremely positive rather than extremely negative:

> Ernestina took the ivory-topped pencil from the top of the diary and struck through March 26th. It still had nine hours to run, but she habitually allowed herself this little cheat. . . . Some fifteen pages in . . . there came a blank, upon which she had pressed a sprig of jasmine . . . the day she had thought she would die of joy, had cried endlessly, the ineffable . . . (5)

Often, in this way, Fowles connects timelessness with exaltation. At the end of the novel, when Charles has *his* moment of eternal bliss, time is again brought to an impossible halt. The traditionally romantic ending closes with Charles and Sarah sharing an eternal moment of timelessness and transcendence. The eternal moment has two main characteristics: it is very rare and very transitory. These features distinguish it from the eternal now, which instead is a feeling of a duration of presentness at the expense of the past/future. At the end of the "happy" ending Fowles stresses both the rareness and the transcendence of the eternal moment. He tends to associate timelessness with silence, the unutterable, the "ineffable." There is a transcendence of words, language, thought, logic, analysis, of the sober common sense of quotidian time:

> . . . her look [was] unbearably naked. Such looks we have all once or twice in our lives received and shared; they are those in which worlds melt, pasts dissolve, moments when we know, in the resolution of profoundest need, that the rock of ages can never be anything else but love, here, now, in these two hands' joining, in this blind silence in which one head comes to rest beneath the other. . . . (60)

This passage is obviously somewhat sentimentally awkward, and deliberabely so, since it functions as an ironic comment on abandoned literary conventions. Its conception of timelessness is quite relevant, though, and fits in nicely with Fowles's descriptions elsewhere of the eternal moment. Two pages earlier Fowles described this moment with even greater precision. There is a strong emphasis on the idea of time having come to an abrupt halt, of a drastic breach in the quotidian experience

of temporal progression. One notices how Fowles enjoys toying
with time. Playfully he breaks silence with music. Playfully the
idea of a time stop is counterpointed by the opposite notion of
temporal fluidity. Playfully the word *time* is brought to our attention. Playfully the serene atmosphere of timelessness is broken, *while it continues to go on,* by a disturbing and deflating lack
of rhythm and time in the physical background. Playfully
Charles is shown playing with his watch as he had done once
before with the daughter of that other Sarah:

> . . . absorbed by the watch, the child too was silent. In some
> distant house an amateur, a lady with time on her hands—
> not in them, for the execution was poor, redeemed only by
> distance—began to play the piano: a Chopin mazurka,
> filtered through walls, through leaves and sunlight. Only that
> jerkily onward sound indicated progression. Otherwise it was
> the impossible: History reduced to a living stop, a photo-
> graph in flesh. (60)

In the endless chain of time one single link is broken. This is
enough to destroy time. It becomes possible to enter timelessness. For a few moments the individual is given the privilege to
exist outside and beyond time in a dimension that has a quite
tangible physical and psychological reality.

Often, there is a sudden but very convincing shift toward the
occult and the esoteric. An East German Egyptologist tells
Daniel Martin of a strange experience. The professor is "not in
the least a believer in the supernatural" (39). Yet when working
in a tomb at sunset he suddenly has "a curious sense of a living
presence that was not his own":

> "I have had this experience again, but never so vividly as
> on that first occasion. It is of a most strange . . . like a broken
> link in time."
> "A dislocation?"
> "Yes. Thank you. That is a better word. For a little interval
> time does not seem to exist. One is neither the original
> painter nor one's own self, a modern archaeologist. If one is
> anything . . . one is the painting. One exists, but it is somehow
> not in time. In a greater reality, behind the illusion we call
> time. One was always there. There is no past or future. . . .
> This is not to do with mysticism. It is almost physical, some-
> thing hidden in the nature of things. I once had a similar

experience, also after many hours of work, with a difficult papyrus. I became the papyrus, I was beyond time." (39)

Here there is not only a breakdown of time but also of the barrier between subject and object ("one is the painting"; "I became the papyrus"). This follows hours of creative work, of sustained identification, and it resembles those passages, especially in *Daniel Martin,* where the dissolving membrane between narrator and character (and between author and narrator) completely disappears. When Dan and Jane come to the rock tombs where the professor had had his first experience of timelessness, Dan has himself a very disturbing feeling that lasts for a few seconds. Again the balance between the subjective and objective is unsettled. Dan is removed from time but above all from reality. Here it is not a question, as with the eternal now, of entering a reality that is presentness, but of actually being strangely alienated from present reality:

> Then he had a very peculiar few moments of disorientation. Perhaps there really was some *genius loci,* though his experience was not of timelessness, but of somehow being outside his own body, as if he were a camera, merely recording, at a remove from present reality. For a brief but abyss-like space he was not at all sure where he was, what he was doing. This landscape, this voluble guide, the way the wind moved this woman's hair . . . it was like a mechanical trip in the normal current of consciousness, a black-out, an epilepsy, and he found it, during the few seconds it lasted, ominous, unpleasant; as if he, all around him, was an idea in someone else's mind, not his own. (40)

Daniel Martin's plunge into unreality takes place exactly where the professor had entered *his* supernormal dimension. Precisely the same thing happens in *The Magus.* When Nicholas comes to Bourani for the first time, he feels just as Conchis had when *he* came to the timeless island's haunted headland. The intervening years and the separate personal identities matter nothing.

So far we have encountered transitory discontinuations of the time flux. There is an abrupt halt, a stoppage followed by a release into another dimension. After this ephemeral suspension time again moves on and the individual returns unchanged to quotidian time. This is one type of eternal moment. But there is another. In the following out-of-time experiences there is not a flow of time from past to future, discontinued at a specific moment, and then carried on. Instead there is one time stream moving from the past and *another moving from the future*. These arrows of time rush toward each other, and the eternal moment becomes the point where they meet and collide. Past, present, and future become one. The present and the past/future are the same thing. Location is very important: the moment seems to grow out of a particular place. In *The Magus* this is Bourani. In *Daniel Martin* it is Tsankawi:

> I have never quite understood why some places exert this deep personal attraction, why at them *one's past seems in some mysterious way to meet one's future,* one was somehow always to be there as well as being there in reality. . . . In some way, the mesa transcended all place and frontier. . . . There was a sense in which it was a secret place, a literal retreat, an analogue of what had always obsessed my mind; but it also stood in triumphant opposition, and this was what finally, for me, distinguished Tsankawi from the other sites: in them there was a sadness, the vanished past, the cultural loss; but Tsankawi *defeated time,* all deaths. (28; my italics)

In this eternal moment that involves two time-arrows, timelessness and transcendence are not contained within a dark cosmic hole, a precipitous time-gap, but quiver on a superfine point of fulcrum on which the individual's whole life is delicately balanced. Daniel Martin and the professor return to quotidian time after their brief moments of timelessness. Conchis and Nicholas on the other hand are completely shattered. The experience is so intense and unique that it permanently affects their inmost being so as to produce a lasting change of personality. It alters their conceptions of life and time with the sudden illumination of esoteric knowledge. Nicholas's first visit to Bourani is a prelude to what is to come:

> I knocked on the door; the knocks barked sharply over stone floors. But no one came. The house and I waited silently . . . I looked out over the tree-tops and the sea to the languishing ash-lilac mountains . . . a *déjà vu* feeling of having stood in the same place, before that particular proportion of the arches, that particular contrast of shade and burning landscape outside—I couldn't say. (12)

It is from the place itself that everything emanates. Place and hazard. Fowles uses exact clock time as a counterbalancing device that serves at once to pinpoint the miraculous and to deflate what is verging on the occult. Here is Conchis's arrival to the house decades earlier:

> On my last day I had a boatman take me round the island. For pleasure. By chance he landed me for a swim at Moutsa down there. By chance he said there was an old cottage up here. By chance I came up. The cottage was crumbled walls, a litter of stones choken with thorn-ivy. It was very hot. About four o'clock on the afternoon of April the eighteenth, 1928. . . . I had immediately the sensation that I was expected. Something had been waiting there all my life. I stood there, and I knew who waited, who expected. It was myself. I was here and this house was here, you and I and this evening were here, and they had always been here, like reflections of my own coming. It was like a dream. I had been walking towards a closed door, and by a sudden magic its impenetrable wood became glass, through which I saw myself coming from the other direction, the future. . . .
> I knew at once that I must live here. I could not go beyond. It was only here that my past would merge into my future. . . .
> It is what I mean by hazard. There comes a time in each life like a point of fulcrum. At that time you must accept yourself. It is not any more what you will become. It is what you are and always will be. (17)

This whole situation, however, must be seen in the light of Conchis's position as the magus. He conjures up a vision that is based, perhaps, not so much on literal truth as on a determination to reshape Nicholas's mind and consciousness. Nicholas seems quite aware of this: "He did not tell me of his coming to Bourani as a man tells something that chances to occur to him; but far more as a dramatist tells an anecdote where the play requires" (17). The implication is that the astonishing similarity between Nicholas's and Conchis's sensations of a point of fulcrum may, just possibly, be intended to be seen as a trick. Has Conchis merely manipulated his patient/victim? As I see it, both Conchis's and Nicholas's experiences are genuine. The transient moment brings an authentic insight into the nature of existence and selfhood. Certainly I feel that the magic that Nicholas feels is not that of the magus, but that of a higher form of knowledge.

Nicholas's eternal moment comes close to Charles's in *The French Lieutenant's Woman*. In both cases the forward movement of music serves as a time-marking foil for the out-of-time nature of the moment. It is at this moment that Nicholas begins to understand Conchis and to grasp the secret meaning of the strange notion of meeting one's future:

> It came to me as I listened that I didn't want to be anywhere else in the world at that moment, that what I was feeling at that moment justified all I had been through, because all I had been through *was* my being there. Conchis had spoken of meeting his future, of feeling his life balanced on a fulcrum, when he first came to Bourani. I was experiencing what he meant; a new self-acceptance, a sense that I had to be this mind and this body, its vices and its virtues, and that I had no other chance or choice. (27)

Those last words, "no other chance or choice," are strange words to come from the pen of a man so preoccupied with freedom and existentialism. Much later in *The Magus* there is another, rather different, out-of-time experience that involves fate, self-awareness, *choice*. Conchis had come to play an important part during the German occupation of the island. As the official mayor he had been given the symbolic role of executing two captured freedom fighters in front of the assembled crowd of village hostages. At the crucial moment he is given a choice: he can club the terrorists to death with an unloaded gun; or he can have the eighty hostages shot. The moment is eternalized. He feels removed to a dimension where all is grasped "in a matter of seconds." In the quivering transience of these "fifteen seconds" his whole life resolves itself into a point of fulcrum. His impending decision is set to diffuse its reality, or unreality, over the varied expanse of his entire life span. In the depths of his being Conchis knows that he is about to assume, in this moment of infinite significance, a commitment to something that transcends quotidian time. Strangely, all this is embodied in the desperate suicidal masochism of one anonymous Greek rebel:

> He was the immalleable, the essence, the beyond reason, beyond logic, beyond civilization, beyond history. He was not God, because there is no God we can know. But he was a proof that there is a God that we can never know. . . . All I

saw I saw in a matter of seconds, *perhaps not in time at all.* Saw
that I was the only person left in that square who had the
freedom left to choose, and that the annunciation and de-
fence of that freedom was more important than common
sense, self-preservation, yes, than my own life, than the lives
of the eighty hostages. . . . all I have to set against their
crucified faces are those few transcendent seconds of knowledge. But knowledge like a white heat. . . .
   I stood there perhaps fifteen seconds—I could not tell you,
time means nothing in such situations—and then I dropped the
gun and stepped beside the guerilla leader. (53; my italics)

It appears, then, that we have two distinct types of point-of-
fulcrum experience. One involves choice—is choice. The other
is the very opposite of choice—a sense of absolute destiny. In
the first type the single time-line comes to a crucial point at
which it splits up into two diverging routes. In the second type
two time lines converge at the point of destiny. We have seen in
The French Lieutenant's Woman how Fowles allows Charles
Smithson to pursue two separate courses of action as the plot
reaches a crucial fork. This is the first type of equilibrium: a
suspension is created by an outward, centrifugal motion, where
two potential futures hold the now between them. In the second type of equilibrium there is a crushing, centripetal suction
of the individual into the dark swallowing funnel of a now.
Here the past and future rush toward each other with forces so
evenly matched that man, left for a few seconds undisturbed in
the serene center of some vast cosmic whirlpool, can briefly
contemplate the nature of his own existence before being re-
lentlessly swept on by the conflicting currents of an enigmatic
reality.
   Strangely, or perhaps significantly, *The Magus* ends with a
point-of-fulcrum experience where the centrifugal and centripetal types of moment seem to coexist within a single now.
There is both "fission and fusion." There is choice; but no
choice is ever made. All is hazard. Balancing on the narrow rim
of a terrifying now between all his past and his future, the
protagonist will plunge in one direction or the other, and this
decisive movement will not be the outcome of conscious will-
power but of an involuntary gesture, a mere flick of time. The
idea of being caught between one's entire past and one's entire
future is first adumbrated in the image of a plate that Nicholas
happens to break right down the middle. He looks at the two

pieces and recognizes the accidental symbolism, the tokens of an impersonal destiny: "My life, my past, my future" (77). This image leads up to the final meeting between Nicholas and Alison in Regents Park, an encounter that is in itself a point of converging time lines: the parallel with Conchis's meeting with Lily during the First World War is stunning. For Nicholas it is Alison who now must choose between him and the Conchis set. For Alison it is Nicholas who must choose between resuming his past life and changing into something better, less selfish. After all he has gone through on the island, including the ultimate deception of being made to believe that Alison had committed suicide, Nicholas feels he has had enough. Without any premeditation at all he slaps her right across the face. The point of fulcrum here is one in which Nicholas senses that the seconds that follow hold the key to their entire future. The balance between man and woman, past and future, love and hate, integration and disintegration, independence and interdependence, is so fine that the slightest chance word or gesture will thrust them one way or the other:

> We stared wildly at each other for a long moment, in a kind of terror: the world had disappeared and we were falling through space. . . .
> The final truth came to me, as we stood there, trembling, searching, between all our past and all our future; at a moment when the difference between fission and fusion lay in a nothing, a tiniest movement, betrayal, further misunderstanding. (78)

As we shall see in the following chapter, the indeterminacy of such situations is derived from a very special Fowlesian way of relating time, space, and reality to each other.

9 Space-time and Reality

The words of the language as they are written or spoken do not seem to play any role in my mechanism of thought, which relies on more or less clear images of a visual and some of a muscular type.

Albert Einstein

In *The Magus* Conchis shows Nicholas a painting of a girl drying herself in front of a mirror: "It was an unforgettable painting; it set a dense golden halo of light round the most trivial of moments, so that the moment, and all such moments, could never be completely trivial again" (15). This echoes the moment in *The French Lieutenant's Woman* when Charles is carried by the song of a wren into "a far deeper and stranger reality," and where the narrator mentions a painting by Pisanello "that catches exactly such a moment" (29). Art is again emphasized as Conchis shows Nicholas a smiling stone face from the sixth or seventh century before Christ. There has been an argument about progress. Nicholas sees his time as a dark age reaching its frightening peaks in Belsen and Hiroshima. To dispel his rigid nihilism Conchis brings in this fragment of sculpture. It is a symbol of a faith in life that transcends the specific evil of a particular time:

> The eyes were faintly oriental, long, and as I saw, for Conchis put a hand over the mouth, also smiling. The mouth was beautifully modelled, timelessly intelligent and timelessly amused.
> "That is the truth. Not the hammer and sickle. Not the stars and stripes. Not the cross. Not the sun. Not gold. Not *yin* and *yang*. But the smile." (23)

Like the eternal moment, art creates transcendence. Art is timeless; conquers time. The smile is "timelessly intelligent and timelessly amused."

The highest levels of Fowles's art are concerned with this transcendence, with what Daniel Martin calls "the methods of conquering time" (39). When he returns to Oxford, he enjoys seeing the old familiar places and faces. But he feels also "something much deeper than that, the strange reversals of time, of personal histories . . . moments that you are glad, for once, to have survived to" (15). While Anthony is dying, Dan rediscovers the lost intimacy of their youth: "there was something—an unchangingness, behind all the outward shifts of circumstance. Time lay quiescent, if not defeated" (17). A few hours before his suicide Anthony asks Dan to love Jane:

> And for a few moments, but once again moments of that hinged, geometric nature that *destroys time* and conscious notion of sequence, the two men sought something, a mystery and an understanding of it, in each other's eyes. A code of intercourse was being broken, another proposed; and Dan, if he could not grasp its full significance consciously, knew that whatever the state of Anthony's specific faith, he retained a far deeper one in a universal absolute. His seeming obliviousness to time, interval, to all the outward rest, was in fact a mere function of that: what I ask is *timeless* . . . a preposterous but true, demand of personal moral being. (17; my italics)

When Dan gets back from hospital and hears about Anthony's suicide, the unreality of the event is seen against a close spatial and temporal reality. It is impossible to understand "that one could be eternally deprived of another human being so close in space, immediate in time" (19). There is nothing especially unusual or exciting in the way Fowles brings time, space, and reality together here. For this excitement, and for a more profound understanding of the particularly Fowlesian apprehension of transcendence through dimensional interaction, we must turn to certain passages in *The Magus*, which evoke an atmosphere of stellar infinity and cosmic mystery. Conchis claims that he can "travel to other worlds" (17). He is suggesting both a spatial and temporal movement, and he is not speaking in images:

> "I have lived a great deal in other centuries."
> "You mean in literature?"
> "In reality." (17)

Later he gives Nicholas a pamphlet called *On Communication
with Other Worlds*. Here time is a prison. The only way of conquering time and escaping from this prison is a mysterious
form of communication somehow taking place in a timeless
dimension outside quotidian time: "Only one method of communication is not dependent on time" (30). The vastness of
space and time lock man in a microscopic space/time cell within
the cosmos.

ON COMMUNICATION WITH OTHER WORLDS

> To arrive at even the nearest stars man would have to
> travel for millions of years at the speed of light. Even if we
> had the means to travel at the speed of light we could not go
> to, and return from, any other inhabited area of the universe
> in any one lifetime. . . . We are for ever isolated, or so it
> appears, in our little bubble of time. (30)

This bubble of quotidian time is the caged mind of man in the
cul-de-sac of the twentieth century. There is only one way out: to
achieve a spaceless and timeless transcendence. Repeatedly in
Fowles, time and space are related to a third, elusive dimension,
"Reality," to form a cosmographic triangle. There is a passage
which suggests that Fowles is consciously thinking in terms of
such a cosmological trinity. This is the moment of Nicholas's
first experience of Greece:

> It was like a journey into space. I was standing on Mars,
> knee-deep in thyme, under a sky that seemed never to have
> known dust or cloud. . . . I had just written a letter to Alison,
> but already she seemed far away, *not in distance, not in time, but
> in* some dimension for which there is no name. *Reality,* per-
> haps. (7; my italics)

The trivial world of everyday existence vanishes, becomes unreality. This shapes itself as a movement in time as well as in
space:

> . . . the B.B.C. Overseas Service . . . seemed to come from the
> moon . . . while the rare newspapers from England that I saw
> became more and more like their own "One hundred years
> ago today" features. The whole island seemed to feel this
> exile from contemporary reality. (8)

Just as Conchis's pseudoscientific pamphlet speaks of the earth as floating in ghastly interstellar isolation like a "little bubble of time," so Conchis's minature earth and society, this magic island of Prospero's, is a bubble of eerie and timeless unreality. Nicholas feels this metaphysical and dimensional exile quite as clearly as he feels the geographical and cultural alienation, and when he gets a glimpse of the United States Mediterranean fleet on the horizon, space, time, and reality are once more brought into curious patterns of interaction. Through a direction in space ("the south") the disturbance of reality becomes a disturbance of time:

> Death machines holding thousands of gum-chewing, contraceptive-carrying men, for some reason *more thirty years away than thirty miles; as if we were looking into the future, not the south;* into a world where there were no more Prosperos, no private domaines, no poetries, fantasies, tender sexual promises . . . I stood between the two girls and felt acutely the fragility not only of the old man's extraordinary enterprise, but of time itself. (47; my italics)

There is a recurring reference in these recent quotations to heavenly bodies ("stars," "Mars," "the moon"). When Conchis tells Nicholas about his life during the First World War, there comes a break. Nicholas looks up at the sky. Again the feeling of unreality is one in which distance in time is related to distance in cosmic space: "I lay in my chair and stared up at the stars. 1914 and 1953 were aeons apart; 1914 was on a planet circling one of those furthest faintest stars. The vast stretch, the pace of time" (18).

This stellar motif is carried to its furthest point at the end of chapter 36. Conchis hypnotizes the intoxicated protagonist by asking him to look at the star *alpha* Lyrae straight above them. While Nicholas watches the star and gradually falls deeper and deeper into various stages of a hypnotic trance, Fowles shapes Nicholas's dream into a sweeping vision of a series of cosmic landscapes. Space itself is seen through various symbolic perspectives that create disturbingly strange vistas of infinite consciousness and insight. In this evocation of an inner journey that ultimately leads to an awesome moment of transcendent being, the space–time–reality concept is once more carefully worked out. The immersion in a dimension of higher reality involves a simultaneous weakening of the space and time dimensions. First, there is a consciousness of a higher reality, an "awareness of pure being . . . a pure awareness. . . . I had the sense that this was the fundamental reality . . . I suddenly knew, but in a new hitherto unexperienced sense of knowing, that all else exists. . . . There was no meaning. Only being."

Space and time vanish in this "present state, this state without dimensions." There is now a weakening of the space dimension leading to utter *spacelessness*. We see this in a variety of ways. First the word *void* is used as Nicholas glimpses a black anti-space: the observed star is "not one of a pattern of stars, but itself, floating in the blue-black breath of space, in a kind of void . . . breeding and needing the void around it . . . a related sense that I was exactly the same, suspended in a dark void." Second, there is a complete inversion of space, an eversion of the whole cosmos: "Then came a strange illusion; that I was not looking up, but down into space, as one looks down a well." Third, Nicholas senses a wind in the void blowing on him *from all directions at the same time*. Spacelessness is the negative infinity of a cosmic void, universal nothingness:

> There was the glistening, listening void; darkness and expectation. Then there came a wind on my face, a perfectly physical sensation. I tried to face it, it was fresh and warm, but I suddenly realized, with an excited shock, not at anything but the physical strangeness of it, that it was blowing on me from all directions at the same time. I raised my hand, I could feel it. (36)

In the centripetal, spaceless transcendence of this "dark wind breathing in on me from every side," time and timelessness, transience and unchangingness, merge in a reality where the "becoming and the being" are one. All distinctions dissolve and disappear. There is a transcendence of temporal, spatial, ethical, and aesthetic dualisms, even of words and language:

> There was no word . . . I was a recipient. But once again there came this strange surprise that the emitters stood all around me. I was not receiving from any one direction, but from all directions; though once again, direction is too physical a word. I was having feelings that no language based on concrete physical objects, on actual feeling, can describe. I think I was aware of the metaphoricality of what I felt. I knew

words were like chains, they held me back; and like walls with holes in them. Reality kept rushing through. . . . That reality was endless interaction. No good, no evil; no beauty, no ugliness. No sympathy, no antipathy. But simply interaction. (36)

Fowles's novels mirror the unresolvable conflicts of consciousness, but also the revolt against this unresolvability. The novels are all structured so as to allow totally different and opposed strands of time and reality to interpenetrate in a multileveled paradigm of interlocking orders. Through this interaction the reader or protagonist is to become unsettled and roused. The reader of *The Collector* is first asked to believe in reality as Clegg sees it; then, in the second half, to believe in Miranda's version. In *The French Lieutenant's Woman* the intrusive narrator comments on the discrepancy between Charles's and Sarah's ways of looking upon their relationship. Yet the trifurcation, or double bifurcation, of the plot forces the reader himself to choose between temporal incompatibilities. Also, as we have seen, the reader is continuously hurled in time between the fictional Victorian reality of the characters and the slightly more real reality of the twentieth-century narrator. This narrator is in himself an arresting feature in the constant oscillation between fiction and reality. He holds an intermediary position, not by being suspended in the limbo between the author's real world and the imaginary world of his art, but by belonging to them both. The voice of the narrator has very much the extrafictional tone of the person we meet in *The Aristos:* John Fowles himself, the real living man. This, at least, seems to be the intention behind deflating remarks like "I was nosing recently round the best kind of secondhand bookseller's . . ." (39). These casual intrusions and the large amount of documentary material give the narrator a factual image, an impression of really being there, beside the reader, in objective reality. In the following passage the words *I* and *myself* are supposed to make the reader think of Fowles the living writer, not of Fowles the narrator. Whether Fowles actually does own a teapot and jug like those purchased by Sarah when she lived at Endicott's Family Hotel in Exeter matters little. What is important here is the effect that Fowles wishes to create:

She began with a Staffordshire teapot . . . and then a Toby jug, . . . a delicate little thing in pale mauve and primrose-yellow, the jolly man's features charmingly lacquered by a soft blue glaze (ceramic experts may recognize a Ralph Wood). Those two purchases had cost Sarah ninepence in an old china shop; the Toby was cracked, and was to be re-cracked in the course of time, as I can testify, having bought it myself a year or two ago for a good deal more than the three pennies Sarah was charged. But unlike her, I fell for the Ralph Wood part of it. She fell for the smile. (36)

There is of course an immense detachment in the minute care with which the author brings his own plane of reality in line with that of his heroine. One cannot help admiring how Fowles manages, in this crude intrusion, not only to contrast reality with fiction and one time plane with another, but also to link them together in the image of a jug that "was to be recracked in the course of time." The "was to" seems to emphasize some-thing deterministic in the relentless onward movement of time from Sarah's Victorian now to her creator's creative now. It is as if she had created him, instead of vice versa. The cracks become visible externalizations of temporal nerves running from the nineteenth to the twentieth century, from Sarah Woodruff to John Fowles.

The narrator in *The French Lieutenant's Woman*, then, is some-times John Fowles, a person existing in quotidian time, in the everyday reality of the reader—a reality where one strolls casu-ally into old shops and where the narrator's flattering confidential expertise creates an atmosphere of intellectual man-to-man intimacy. Yet while the narrator somehow appears to have a higher than average reality, he is also to a higher than normal degree part of the fictional world, for toward the end of the novel he suddenly turns up as one of its characters: a bearded man, the face "only too familiar to me," enters Charles's first class railway compartment and stares coldly and unpleasantly at him (55). This inchoate narrator-character eventually tosses a coin to determine through hazard which reality is to conclude the novel:

> I cannot give both versions at once, yet whichever is the sec-ond will seem, so strong is the tyranny of the last chapter, the final, the "real" version.
> I take my purse from the pocket of my frock coat, I extract a florin, I rest it on my right thumbnail, I flick it, spinning, two feet into the air and catch it in my left hand.
> So be it. And I am suddenly aware that Charles has opened his eyes and is looking at me. (55)

Fowles here forces us to face four realities: the reality of the first ending, the reality of the second ending, the reality of the narrator-author of 1967, and the reality of the narrator-character of 1867. In these twin sets the alternatives are equally matched, equally valid. The novelist and his characters exist on the same plane, and this is not one of reality but of unreality. In the very first ending preceding the final bifurcation Fowles argues that we are all novelists (45). In his first major intrusion, a brief lecture on fiction and reality, he writes that all novelists

> *wish to create worlds as real as, but other than the world that is.* Or was. . . . It is only when our characters and events begin to disobey us that they begin to live. When Charles left Sarah on her cliff edge, I ordered him to walk straight back to Lyme Regis. But he did not; he gratuitously turned and went down to the Dairy. . . . the idea seemed to me to come clearly from Charles, not myself. . . .
>
> I have disgracefully broken the illusion? No. My characters still exist, and in a reality no less, or no more, real than the one I have just broken. . . . I find this new reality (or unreality) more valid . . .
>
> But this is preposterous? A character is either "real" or "imaginary"? If you think that, *hypocrite lecteur,* I can only smile. You do not even think of your own past as quite real; you . . . fictionalize it . . . put it away on a shelf—your book, your romanced autobiography. We are all in flight from the real reality. That is a basic definition of *Homo sapiens.* (13)

The realities are on a par. The pessimistic/realistic ending is no more plausible or authentic than the optimistic/romantic one, for the universe is thought godless, the world impersonal, reality indifferent. Thus the worlds meet, the unrealities touch each other to form a new, intermediary reality where the author has become character (Fowles tossing a coin in the train) and the character his own author—the whole first ending is not the creation, it is said, of the narrator but of Charles's daydreaming mind:

> . . . the last few pages you have read are not what happened, but what he spent the hours between London and Exeter imagining might happen. . . .
>
> Above all he felt himself coming to the end of a story; and to an end he did not like. If you noticed in those last two chapters an abruptness . . . a small matter of his being given a life span of very nearly a century and a quarter . . . then do

not blame me; because all these feelings, or reflections of
them, were very present in Charles's own mind. The book of
his existence, so it seemed to him, was about to come to a
distinctly shabby close. (45)

For all its unreality the book is still real. For all its reality man's
life is still a book, still fiction, unreality.

Time, once more, is crucial. Charles's false identity is given
an unreal life span of nearly a century and a quarter. In the
coin-tossing scene the narrator exists simultaneously in the
nineteenth and twentieth centuries. First he can say that he has
"pretended to slip back into 1867; but of course that year is in
reality a century past" (55). Then, still in the now of his twentieth-century plotting, he can take not a shilling from his
trouser pocket but a florin from the purse in his frock coat.

The Ebony Tower is full of these games. In the first story one of
the girls is reading *The Magus*. In "The Enigma" the characters
pretend that they are characters: "Let's pretend everything . . .
even you and me sitting here now, is in a novel. . . . Somewhere
there's someone writing us, we're not real."

In *Mantissa* this playfulness runs amock so as to take over and
become the leading theme as Fowles's lashing wit explodes the
sacramental dogma of pseudo-criticism. Having joined the
mandarin caste of ultra-respectable novelists Miles Green carries his novel much as the emperor wears his new clothes in the
fable, only in reversed allegory: Green fancies he is wearing an
invisible nontext only to find that its unreality is unreal, its
invisibility invisible. In this supremely visible text, this shock-
ingly real reality, it is not a question of author intruding into
text, but of text intruding upon author: "What you forget," says
the muse Erato, "is that I am *not* something in a book. I am
supremely real" (II). Indeed the muse transcends, when she
feels so inclined, the temporality of text so as to achieve a mis-
chievous extra-textual existence within the novelist's (Fowles's
and Green's) temporal reality. In a six-week interruption in the
typing of the manuscript Erato has, like a naughty sylph,
slipped out of the text and explored the choice items of pornography in the author's bookshelves:

> "I somehow assumed you would have all the pornographic
> classics by heart."
> "Might I ask how, in your few pages of existence, you
> happen to—"

"Oh Miles!" She gives a hurried smile down. "Really. I thought we were speaking outside the illusions of text." She looks up again. "I mean, take just that one time when, as Dr. Delfie, I asked you why you didn't just get off the bed and leave the room. In reality you took six weeks before you could find an answer. I had to do something while I waited. I felt that at the very least I should familiarize myself with the kind of book evidently dearest to your heart." She adds, "As your employee. So to speak." (II)

In *The Magus* Nicholas soon realizes that Conchis is prepared to go very far in order to wipe out the borderline between reality and unreality. At first, therefore, the sudden appearance of very authentic-looking soldiers in German uniforms has little effect on him. He knows Conchis is trying to destroy his sense of reality by destroying his sense of time: when Lily/ Julie turned up in old clothes he was supposed to think he was back in World War I; now it is World War II. He knows, however, that reality is now. Reality is 1953. Then there is real violence. He is taken prisoner. Suddenly he does not know what to believe. The reader too is totally bewildered as Nicholas is joined by another "captured terrorist":

> ... I saw, with a sharp sense that the masque was running out of control, that he was barefoot. His stumbling, ginger walk was real, not acted. . . . His face was atrociously bruised, puffed, the whole of one side covered in blood from a gash near the right eye. . . . Without warning the soldier behind jabbed him savagely in the small of the back. I saw it, I saw his spasmic jerk forward, and the—or so it sounded—absolutely authentic gasp of pain the jab caused. . . . I knew by then where I was. I was back in 1943, and looking at captured resistance fighters. (49)

A gauge of Nicholas's sense of unreality here is the fact that he finds comfort in the stale taste of the cigarettes that one of the soldiers gives him. They taste 1943. In 1943 they would have tasted *now:* "The younger soldier felt in his tunic top-pocket and tossed me down three cigarettes. . . . Along each one was printed in red, between little black swastikas, the words *Leipzig dankt euch.* The one I smoked tasted very stale, at least ten years old . . . In 1943 it would have tasted fresh" (49). Once more the Conchis-Nicholas relationship parallels the narrator-character relationship in *The French Lieutenant's Woman.* The nauseatingly

omniscient and omnipotent god of this timeless and spaceless
Greek masque is, like the pseudo-author of that other, Victorian, god game, a bit too clever, a bit too ingenious. But this
arrogance is conscious—a quite deliberate prodding at the
phlegmatic nerves and intellectual apathy of the sluggish
reader floating away in the dulling comfort of a fictional
dreamworld. In *The Magus* it is a prodding at the pseudo-
existentialist stance of a protagonist whose life is one of unreality—of narcissism and self-indulgence. The god games, we see,
are time games. Nicholas jumps back a decade as the soldier
tosses cigarettes to him. The reader of *The French Lieutenant's
Woman* jumps back a century as Fowles tosses a Victorian florin
for him. In both cases we learn something about the unreality
of all reality.

Fowles's novels depict a man or woman in the intoxicating
process of gaining a higher order of reality (transcendence) or
in the disintoxicating process of regaining reality (self-
knowledge).

These two processes may be examined separately; they tend
to appear, however, in simultaneous coexistence. Nicholas, the
individual selected by hazard, journeys from the quotidian time
of a trivial reality to a higher reality of cosmic transcendence
and timelessness. At the same time, though, there is a downward movement. The unreality of his false self is broken down
and destroyed by the more powerful unreality of the masque.
This unreality takes him to a soaring summit of romance, fan-
tasy, and magic, only to plunge him cruelly to a solid bedrock of
sober reality. Time is repeatedly linked to the image of reality
bursting through, and this may refer to either of the two processes. When Nicholas strains "back through time to seize Alison" (60), he is trying to see her as an ordinary person within
quotidian time instead of as an elusive ghost within the
timelessness and unreality of Conchis's masque; but when Conchis speaks of his visits to Seidevarre in northern Scandinavia,
"a place I do not want time to touch" (45), the conquest of time
is related to the opposite process of gaining access to a higher,
mystical reality. Like the raving madness of the masque, the
insanity of Henrik, the religious maniac, promotes sanity in the
spectator. Here, on the banks of an Arctic river, "a mirror
unlooked-in since time began" (44), one is, as on Phraxos,
forced through unreality to face reality—but in a totally differ-

ent sense. The reality that bursts through here is sublime and elevating. There is no fall to a firm bed-rock following the loss of delusion. This *is* delusion—frightening not because of its unreality, but because of its reality.

> He . . . knelt on the shingle. . . . Something was very close to him. . . . I would have given ten years of my life to have been able to look out there to the north, from inside his mind. I did not know what he was seeing, but I knew it was something of such power, such mystery, that it explained all. . . . He was not waiting to meet God. He was meeting God . . .
>
> Up to this point in my life . . . my whole approach was scientific, medical, classifying. . . .
>
> But in a flash, as of lightning, all our explanations, all our classifications and derivations, our aetiologies, suddenly appeared to me like a thin net. That great passive monster, reality, was no longer dead, easy to handle. It was full of a mysterious vigour, new forms, new possibilities. The net was nothing, reality burst through it. . . . I could offer no consolation. . . . There are situations in which consolation only threatens the equilibrium that time has instituted. (44)

In Fowles's different novels the protagonist finds himself in a situation that forces him to remove a barrier between himself and reality. This situation is one of sudden loneliness. The reality that usually surrounds the individual disappears completely: Miranda suddenly alone with herself in Clegg's cellar; Nicholas suddenly abandoned by all the actors in the masque; Charles suddenly outside the whole Victorian establishment, even despised by Sarah . . . an outcast having to face the "unplumb'd, salt, estranging sea"; Daniel Martin alone with himself in the Middle East, holding out a hand to Jane . . . in vain. As the unreal is made to mingle with the real, the individual is forced to define and redefine reality. As surface reality slips from his hold, he tightens his grip on that innermost selfhood that lies emotionally intact within the deepest recesses of each conscious mind. There is in *Daniel Martin* a moment of such a regaining of reality that takes place, just as in Conchis's masque, through the theatrical. This is when Dan notices a tramp rummaging below his hotel window: "There was something obscurely comic about him . . . and something *Victorian, anachronistic,* almost *timeless.* He was both very real and, under the street-lights, on the empty stage of the night, theatrical.

Beckett again, and waiting for Godot" (20; my italics). Like the
vagabonds in Beckett's time-warped drama, this tramp reflects
man's life as an unreal acting concealing extreme inner solitude
and estrangement. He is theatrical. Yet somehow his unreality
contains a timeless core of truth that makes it much more bear-
able than the unreality of the social games that Daniel Martin
has been forced to play. As in *The Magus,* theatrical unreality
illuminates for the protagonist the lack of reality in his life. Dan
feels like asking the tramp up for a cup of coffee just in order to

> regain reality in a day that had somehow cast Dan himself as
> unreal: too full of polite lies, unnatural smiles and urbanities,
> conventional middle-class behaviors. All through it he had
> felt like someone locked up inside an adamantly middle-class
> novel. . . . Dan imagined that he was looking at his lost real
> self down there, in that shadowy figure; a thing living on the
> edge of existence in a night street of his psyche; beyond
> conversation and invitation, eternally separate.
>   But then, as he watched, he was returned to theater
> again. . . . The tramp . . . lifted aside a bundle in the pram for
> the policeman to see something underneath, and they
> seemed to discuss it. The tramp even lifted it a little, so Dan
> could see: an old wall-clock, rejected time. (20)

The real self is, as in *The French Lieutenant's Woman,* a self of
fundamental enislement. The regaining of reality is very much
a question of abandoning relationships, and especially sexual
relationships, that promote an escape from the understanding
of one's permanent freedom and isolation.

This may seem a rather hasty conclusion, since there is in the
novels a movement toward, and not only away from, the sexual
relationship. In each of the three major novels there is a pair of
women in which one stands for escape and the other for the
regaining of reality. In *The Magus* Lily/Julie represents unreality and Alison reality, although the initial swing is from Alison
to Lily/Julie, from the prosaic to the mysterious. In *The French
Lieutenant's Woman* Ernestina belongs to unreality, to a world
that is shallow, false and dead compared with Sarah's. The
realistic/romantic dualism is inverted here: it is the "romantic"
Sarah who represents reality while Ernestina stands for comfortable escape. In *Daniel Martin* Jenny represents the unreality
of a false eternal now, while Jane possesses a much more authentic ability to dissolve time:

this obscure ex-sister-in-law was someone whose spirit remained not quite like that of any other woman he had ever known . . . there are some people one can't dismiss, place, reify . . . who set riddles one ignores at one's cost; who, like nature itself, are catalytic, inherently and unconsciously *dissolvent of time* and all the naturalist tries to put between himself and his total reality. (33; my italics)

It is not as simple as this of course; not a mere transition from a woman of unreality to a woman of reality. The novels describe not so much a man exchanging one relationship, or one set of relationships, for another, more valid one; the novels show, rather, the beauty and the pain of the process in which a sensitive mind moves from ignorance of self to knowledge of self. The sexual ties are of secondary importance. The "unreal" women are the mere instruments of illusion . . . not in themselves illusion. The "real" women have on closer examination nothing real about them at all. But they become, chiefly unconsciously and involuntarily, instruments of disenchantment and self-knowledge. Believing he is searching for the woman of his life, the protagonist is really undertaking the quest for something far more elusive.

There is, to be sure, freedom; but selfhood being also a terrifying loneliness, this freedom is bitter, fragmentary. In *The French Lieutenant's Woman* Charles finally loses all in order to gain a freedom that is equally frightening and unshared. *Daniel Martin* would seem to be a move in a new direction, since Dan actually ends up by reaching Jane. Yet this is a novel that more than any other is concerned with the self. Here we have not a wavering between two women but between two selves. Between Daniel Martin and Daniel Martin. Or, if you wish, between Daniel Martin and Simon Wolfe.

"Simon Wolfe" is the novel that Dan first wants to write about a fictive character but then decides to write about himself. This is "the most important decision of his life" (32). From the beginning Dan knows that his first attempt at fiction will be a self-portrait. His aim is the real self. Yet he knows that he is an artist, one who must communicate indirectly, one who must convey the real through the unreal, reality through fiction, Daniel Martin through Simon Wolfe. He thinks first of giving Simon Wolfe a darker personality than his own. Then he considers a softer, more rounded identity. Finally he rejects both extremes and decides to paint himself exactly as he is. Only this solution will permit him to "set out for the land that inspired the proposed voyage: himself" (32). "Simon Wolfe" becomes Daniel Martin; and therefore, in a very special sense, Daniel Martin becomes Simon Wolfe: *Daniel Martin,* the novel about a man trying to write a novel, *becomes* that emerging self-study, that growing embryo of "Simon Wolfe." As Simon merges with Dan, so the written *Daniel Martin* blends with the to-be-written "Simon Wolfe." Thus this novel is given a temporal structure that permits its hero to exist simultaneously in the subjective presentness of the observer-novelist and the concluded past of the observed character. Dan decides to abandon the idea of making Simon Wolfe either more negative or more positive than himself:

> . . . a third solution . . . had not occurred to the writer-to-be until this moment. Dan was at the bottom of his orchard by then, just above the stream. There was an obscure scuffle in the hedge to his right; some nocturnal animal. . . . He felt, transitorily . . . a paradoxical sort of determined imprison-ment compared to the existence of the small wild beast he had disturbed; almost an envy of the pleasures of a life with-out self-consciousness.
>   Free will.
>   And then, in those most banal of circumstances . . . he came to the most important decision of his life. It did not arrive . . . in one blinding certainty; but far more as a tenta-tive hypothesis, . . . forgotten through most of the future of these pages. . . . though it may seem a supremely self-centered declaration, it is in fact a supremely socialist one. . . .
>   To hell with cultural fashion; to hell with elitist guilt; to hell with existentialist nausea; and above all, to hell with the imagined that does not say, not only in, but behind the im-ages, the real. (32)

The most striking symbol in the novel is the Egyptian py-ramid. The Pharaoh's effort to conquer time is a dead monu-ment inspired by futile self-absorption. Yet in spite of this Dan gradually comes to agree with the old German professor: artists are "the only true pharaohs left; so let them be their own cele-bratory masons, and return to the self, abandon all the work on the other tombs and monuments" (39).

10   Temporality

The observation and analysis of children skiing now plays almost as large a part in the formulation of ski technique and ski school teaching pro- grammes as that of the world's top ski racers. And comparisons show that *young children and racers ski in remarkably similar ways.* . . . Adults, on the other hand, with their more intellectual approach, are continually attempting to measure their performance against some ideal of perfect technique.
Karl Gamma, The Handbook of Skiing

From the time of Parmenides and Heraclitus metaphysical speculation in the West has polarized views of time and reality as either permanence or change, determinism or free will, necessity or contingency, being or becoming. In literature we find an early reflection of this dichotomy in the differing tem- poral stances of Aeschylus and Euripides.[19] One may define the general, quotidian apprehension of time as the sense of the coexistence of these apparently incompatible aspects of tem- porality: time is conflict, a tension in which man acquires a permanent selfhood, as well as an identity within change by having to endure the unresolvable conflicts of the mind.[20]

The transition from quotidian time to the experience of "timelessness" always involves, in my opinion, a *lessening of ten- sion.* But since we attach opposite values to different experi- ences of timelessness, we cannot discover a meaningful para- digm of time, a hierarchy of specifically human temporalities, by bunching all experiences of "timelessness" *below* temporal conflict. The hierarchy of temporalities will therefore be based on a crucial discrimination between descendental and tran- scendental timelessness. In a triple-tiered paradigm I shall call descendental timelessness *subtemporality*, middle zone time-as- conflict *quotidian time*, and transcendental timelessness *transtem- porality*. (In chapter 12 *levotemporality* corresponds to what I have here called *quotidian time*, and the descendental and transcendental extremes are depolarized as a parallel or enclosing temporal mood: *dextrotemporality*.)

The Fowlesian protagonist moves *between* these levels of temporality and sustains therefore not only ordinary middle-range tension within quotidian time but also the deeper and far more disturbing tension between the different levels. Thus we have one mind, two cognitive styles, three main levels of temporal habitation and four basic types of existential tension: the first within quotidian time, the second between subtemporality and transtemporality, the third between subtemporality and quotidian time, and the fourth between quotidian time and transtem-

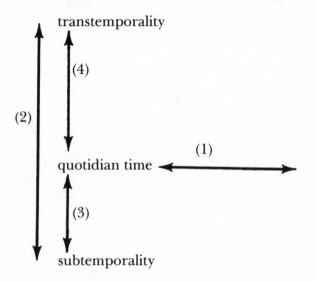

porality. I shall try to show that an awareness of such a paradigmatic discrimination is a prerequisite for making sense of the body of endless temporal subtleties in Fowles's fiction, and for understanding consciousness in general. I now turn to the various tensions to examine them in the sequence in which they have been listed above.

In *The French Lieutenant's Woman* Charles Smithson experiences in an intensified form the universal quotidian sense of time as conflict (the first tension). Being both a fossil and a collector of fossils, belonging simultaneously to the world of absolute permanence (feudalism) and the world of pure change (capitalism), Charles endures in the middle ground of his daily life that coexistence of temporal incompatibilities which is for all of us the minute-by-minute tension (1) of ordinary human life. There is hazard as well as choice, freedom within unfreedom. There is both being and becoming, for Charles changes by being: he moves by refusing to move with others; he travels in time by refusing to move with time. The salvation and the crucifixion are one.

In his flights from quotidian conflict within the dark Victorian time-bubble Charles is torn (the second tension) between the double attraction of descendental and transcendental timelessness and comes, therefore, to sustain a new temporal conflict. The dulling pull of an easy return to *sub*temporality manifests itself in the false eternal now of his ancestral grounds, as well as in the artificial ecstasy of the urban underworld, culminating in his spewing as the unravished prostitute gives her name as "Sarah." The magnetic pull of a magic but painful climb into an equally time-defeating *trans*temporality is reflected in the sublime eternal now of the *natural* underworld of the Undercliff, culminating in the transcendent experience of ravishing the "real" Sarah while whispering her name.

Daniel Martin is torn by this same second tension. In his flight from the past/futurity of "Englishness" he is split between the mindless subtemporal libertinism of the Californian jet set and the transtemporality of the Tsankawi Indian, Zen Buddhist, and Egyptian Pharaoh. As we have seen, this ethical perspective of a choice between ostensibly identical releases from temporal conflict is given also an aesthetic dimension in this novel: Daniel Martin can choose the straightforward presentness of cinematic art; but eventually he abandons this for the more complex and profound presentness of a novelistic stucture that aspires to convey a dazzling coexistence and equivalency of experienced nows within an elevated, but culturally lost, level of temporality.

The most fascinating treatment of this second tension occurs in *The Magus*. Here Fowles holds Nicholas Urfe so long in a temporal limbo between subtemporality and transtemporality that the protagonist comes to experience a sustained existential ambiguity, which slowly but insistently asserts itself as the atemporal world of the eerie. When Nicholas comes to Phraxos he is already in flight from the brutal reality of a world in which everything is disappointingly relative and temporal. His fear of perpetual petty conflict within the temporal mediocrity of quotidian time soon becomes pathological. As he sinks into temporal coma, his sense of identity and social belonging is radically diminished. Relationships and selfhood begin to dissolve. Conchis the doctor diagnoses this as a collapse into subtemporality, and the treatment is an overdose of transtemporality. The heavy shocks of transcendental timelessness are implemented by Conchis the magus in order to restore the healthy intermediate level of human life as suffering and active love.

Whereas quotidian time is characterized by the sense of a necessary and sustained tension between enduring and rejecting the past, the present, and the future, regressive subtemporality implies a one-sided identification with the past as guilt, the present as magic, and the future as death.[21] Nicholas's preoccupation with guilt (Alison and all the reminders of the past), magic (Lily and all the acausal erotic sequences of the masque), and death (Conchis and all his death games: Russian roulette, Nazi executions, and so forth) is obvious. Yet what is perhaps less obvious is that whereas the *magical* reality of the novel is derived from tensionless subtemporality, the timelessness of *mystery* that also permeates *The Magus* is qualitatively altogether different, since it grows out of a tension between opposite forms of tensionlessness: Fowles and Conchis hold Nicholas in a breathtaking suspension between the subtemporal and transtemporal (tension 2).

Freud associated *magical* causation with the subtemporal id that roams unrestricted in dreams and insanity; and Jung's *Koinzidenzprincip* with its conception of magical subtemporal synchronicity gives a certain twist to the ostensibly adolescent motif of Conchis's telepathic speculations and experiences.[22] *Mystery*, on the other hand, grows, according to Freud, out of a situation of ambiguity, of doubtful classification: doll/human being, animal/human being, corpse/human being, familiar/unfamiliar.[23]

Nicholas faces many such disturbing phenomena, and they are all triggered by Conchis: he discovers a skull (dehumanized humanity) and a doll (dehumanized Lily and humanized wood) swinging from a pine tree (57); he is baffled by the fact that Lily has a twin sister and that each twin has a double identity; at the trial he confronts a witch, a crocodile-head, a vampire, a monster, a skeleton, a fish-woman-bird, and a jackal-head, as the magus gives the archetypes of the collective unconscious the language of myth; he clashes with the elusive Negro who at first appears to be the island's giant and semibrutish Caliban; he does not know whether Alison is dead or alive; at one point he does not even know if Conchis is alive, for a gravestone in Athens suggests that he has been dead for four years; and finally the *déjà vu* experience of seeing Conchis's villa suggests the mystery of a future that is at once supremely known and unknown. Nicholas experiences the unsettling ambiguity of the mysterious within the tabooed world of marginal creatures that are supernatural by virtue of being superhuman as well as subhuman. As Lily's human identity splits upward and downward from woman into madonna and whore, the middle ground of quotidian time splits up into subtemporality and transtemporality. Nicholas finally settles back into quotidian time, but only when Conchis permits the artificial oscillation between the temporal polarities to lose its insane intensity. The disintoxication of the trial marks the transition from the tension (2) *between* the timeless extremes to the tension (1) *within* the relative world of quotidian time—the transition from the ambiguously alternating, or bisected (idealized/objectified) concept of woman as angel/beast (Lily/Julie) to the integrative living enigma of woman as a complex and contradictory being subject to time and change (Alison).

This illustrates a fundamental law of consciousness and the dangers involved in failing to recognize it: the impossibility of escaping temporal conflict. For, as we have seen, *temporal conflict exists also outside quotidian time.* The reason is that what we think of as "timelessness" is not a monolithic structure, not a simple and safe haven in which to find everlasting refuge, but a multiverse with its own equally harassing and often much more dangerous incompatibilities.

Conchis's metatheater is timeless because his actors deliberately disregard the unit of time. The psychodrama that enfolds the protagonist is a time-warp play in which there is a triple distortion of time: the dissolutions of quotidian time into (a) descendental magic and (b) transcendental ecstasy, and, in addition, the mystery of (c) temporal ambiguity in between. As the dual aspect of contrasting temporal extremes gives way to one single integrated intermediary level, the various ambiguous figures of the masque remove their masks and abandon their double identities. The unit of time is restored, and the emergence of single identities on the island coincides with Nicholas's rejection of guilt-magic-death and achievement of selfhood.

The novels all trace the protagonist's development toward an acceptance of time as conflict; yet Nicholas, Charles, and Dan move in very different ways through temporal chaos. Daniel Martin comes with Jane to a point of temporal ambiguity which we may easily mistake, without the discriminations of the temporal paradigm for the temporal limbo that Nicholas experiences with Lily (tension 2). In both cases we are cut off from the temporal mainland of quotidian time, but cut off in very different ways. In *The Magus* we are on a Greek island; in *Daniel Martin* in an Arabian desert. While the images of island and desert both suggest a severance from the mainstream of temporal existence, they also suggest vital discrepancies. Dan and Jane feel they are in a weird time-warp play, and this is of course precisely what Conchis's masque is. There is a vast difference, though. Nicholas is torn between subtemporality and transtemporality and loses his grip on reality in the double world of mystery (the second tension). He is surrounded by so many creatures, events, and identities that reality loses its contours through its superfluousness.

Daniel Martin, by contrast, vegetates in the torpid void between subtemporality and quotidian time (the third tension). In the chrysalis larvae collapse into an opaque soup before emerging as butterflies, and it is in such an apparent nothingness that Dan is anguished. In the desolation of *Daniel Martin* the threat of reality is its emptiness, and time often makes itself felt through its absence. One can only wait. Like the mysterious island of Phraxos the Hotel Zenobia of Palmyra is a Salle d'Attente. Significantly, Fowles pinpoints the transition state of this third tension in his selection of Gramsci's "interregnum" for the novel's epigraph.

The Fowlesian protagonist moves toward relationships and identity in quotidian time rather than toward ultimate mysticism and long-range immersion in the transtemporal. There are moments of most phantasmagoric flight, but these are still only moments. At the erotic peaks of each novel sexual fulfillment tends to be a mystical and timeless experience which combines the ecstasy of dance with the ecstasy of transcendent contemplation. A delicate balance (the fourth tension) is struck between quotidian time and transtemporality: men and women move toward sex as a relationship in time while retaining the possibility and memory of sex as a transcendent experience outside time. These existential climaxes, or releases from quo-

tidian conflict, are in themselves not entirely free from a background sense of temporal progression.

In *The French Lieutenant's Woman* Sarah Woodruff is at once
an expression of time and timelessness. For Charles and for the
reader she belongs to time insofar as she represents a new
feminine consciousness founded in the historical beginnings of
female emancipation. Sarah lives in time and fights time. As a
social being she belongs to a temporal and existential avant-
garde. On this social plane her love for Charles exists as a
relationship in time and in a finite reality, and therefore it has
no future, since she and Charles are socially and temporally
incompatible by belonging to different classes and different
centuries. Yet outside time Sarah exists as an equally real reality. As an experience outside society and outside time, Charles's
and Sarah's love for each other is timeless in a number of
senses; and it is in the light of this sustained tension between
the incompatible concepts of time and timelessness that we
must ultimately accept and find significance in the double
bifurcation of the various endings.

In a very different way *The Magus* also ends in a double but
simultaneous expression of reality as time and timelessness. As
in a motion picture that suddenly ends by freezing into a still,
the action is abruptly suspended in an eternal present in which
Nicholas and Alison are for ever moving toward *and* away from
each other in time, as well as remaining perpetually immobile.
As free will and hazard are about to decide their fate, they are
eternally arrested in a split second of time between fission and
fusion: forever being, forever becoming.

In the retrospective and introspective reality of *Daniel Martin*,
Fowles gives this finely apprehended tension a similar aesthetic
twist as a structural tension within the artist's creativity between
the present eternal of time lost and the present progressive of
writing in the hope of retrieving that loss.

This tension between quotidian time and transtemporality is
evoked with great subtlety in each novel at a moment of heightened intensity, when the temporal and transtemporal qualities
of music by chance come to frame a phantom opening perceived in the tapestry of time. The "rise and descent of progressive scales" (6) from a student oboist playing Delius reach
Daniel Martin through the Oxford rain as Jane trails her free
hand across the rug, like a medieval bride, to initiate their *acte
gratuit* outside time. At the end of *The French Lieutenant's Woman*

Charles fumbles hastily for his watch to distract the daughter of that other, real Sarah. Not far away "a lady with time on her hands—not in them" begins to play a Chopin mazurka: only "that jerkily onward sound indicated progression. Otherwise it was the impossible: History reduced to a living stop" (60). In *The Magus* Nicholas listens to "the driving onwardness of Bach, the endless progressions" (27), and suddenly glimpses the meaning of Conchis's words about meeting our future and feeling life balanced on a fulcrum.

11   Untimeliness

C'est le moment où il faut *décider* si nous graverons ce que nous entendons.
Et si graver sauve ou perd la parole.

Jacques Derrida, L'écriture et la différence

In *Mantissa* (1982) time is represented by the Swiss cuckoo clock in the gray hospital room where novelist Miles Green wakes up in a state of severe amnesia. The clock has been left there by Mr. O'Brien—a reference to the Irish comic novelist Flann O'Brien. In Fowles's view *At Swim-Two-Birds* is the first and finest "upsetting of the left-lobe applecart" in fiction. The unit of time, however, is the written or unwritten page: "How long have I been here?" asks the novelist. "Just a few pages," the muse tells him (I). "Pages?" exclaims Green. Later she herself measures the flux of time in pages: "I somehow simply realized, from the very first page of my existence, that I was basically rather a shy person" (II); "I feel so terribly conscious I'm only a few pages old" (II).

The hospital room represents the novelist's mind. Its gray quilted walls represent the gray matter of the human brain. Time in this supremely internalized world is itself internalized as pagination: the ordered sequence of pages, but also the uncontrollable interchangeability of pages in the tides of textuality. Poised on the line of demarcation between text and externality the clock on the wall seems to threaten the novelist's bland composure. Miles Green has retreated so far into the comfortably numb subtemporality of purely fictional time, that the spasmodic ejaculations of quotidian time from the wall become the fearful intrusion of external reality: "He remained staring at the hideous clock: its lunatically cluttered front, its dropped intestines of weights and chains. It did disturb him, standing for something he feared, he couldn't say why; an anomaly, an incongruous reminder of all he could not remember" (I). At the very end the bird in the clock appears one last time "to reaffirm its extraneity, its distance from all that has happened in that room" (IV).

Below the more serious assessment of the predicament of writing as alienation there is the usual Fowlesian toying with time patterns. Anachronisms abound as Fowles allows the temporal orders of writing and discourse to jingle and clash in grotesque dissonance. The muse is caught wearing not only a wristwatch (II) but also the rose "Ophelia," which, according to Green, did not appear until 1923 (it was bred, in fact, by Paul in 1912).[24]

In *Mantissa* Fowles makes fun of the notion that the text writes itself, that the author is nonauthor. Green is a nonauthor. He is an unconscious medium, and when Nurse Cory shows him the text he has written he is utterly uncomprehending. Green journeys from nonauthorship to authorship, from frigidity to satyriasis. His final ithyphallic metamorphosis is the nonauthor's ultimate castration. As nonauthor Green gives the muse the following smug lecture on the poststructuralist novel:

> Serious modern fiction has only one subject: the difficulty of writing serious modern fiction. First, it has fully accepted that it is only fiction . . . and therefore has no business at all tampering with real life or reality. . . . [The true novelist is] not going to waste his time over the messy garage-mechanic drudge of assembling stories and characters on paper. . . . Obviously he has at some point to write something, just to show how irrelevant and unnecessary the actual writing part of it is. But that's all. . . . At the creative level there is in any case no connection whatever between author and text. . . . The deconstructivists have proved that beyond a shadow of doubt. The author's role is purely fortuitous and agential. He has no more significant a status than the bookshop assistant or the librarian who hands the text *qua* object to the reader. . . . Our one priority now is mode of discourse, function of discourse, status of discourse. Its metaphoricality, its disconnectedness, its totally ateleological self-containedness. (II)

Some astronomers argue that an object swallowed by a blackhole in this universe would turn up as an antiobject in the corresponding whitehole of another universe. In this manner the extreme gravitation which pulls Green as nonauthor into the abyss of crypto-Derridean nonpresence thrusts him out on the other side as the negation of the negation, the abyss that is abyssed: "a pleasing intimation of superiority, of having somehow got to the top of the heap" (I). As E. M. Forster showed with Henry James, no author is more present than one who tries to wipe himself right out of the text. The final turn of the screw permits Fowles very craftily to elude the curfew imposed on the free territory of serious fiction by the nihilistic dogmas of a literary vogue. The deconstructivists are outdeconstructed. The self-effacement of nonpresence becomes the presence of blankness. A novel about the antinovel becomes an anti-antinovel.

Behind the multiple insanity of all this looms the sanity of a creative mind that refuses to be impressed by criticism or by self. From the vantage point of the human brain, a padded cell with a cuckoo clock, the free play of authorial intention allows itself to run amok in the labyrinth of the nontext: in the pontifical logocentrism of Miles Green, but also in the indeterminable textuality of *Mantissa*. The literary establishment is hardly viewed in a favorable light. Like Prufrock's evening, criticism's archetypal novelist is a patient etherized upon a table. The twilight of Green's noncreative mind suggests not only the tabula rasa of a faintly illuminated consciousness passively awaiting the impersonal imprint of a self-writing text, but the amnesia, perhaps, of something vaster: of a genre, a subculture—a planet.

With supercilious solemnity and infinite contempt Green dismisses "the positively medieval illusion" (II) that writers write their own books. Yet in the malicious innocence and sheer, irresponsible fun of *Mantissa*, Fowles ironically establishes the supreme autonomy of the free, creative mind, its supreme power to be, as text, exactly what it wants to be. The tables are turned. It is as if Dickens, reading a structuralist essay called "How Successful Is *Hard Times*?" were to sit down and write a novel called *How Successful Is Structuralism?*—which is, of course, exactly what he did in the early 1850s, if by structuralism we mean, not a particular technical approach existing in time (the middle of the twentieth century), but a dehydrated, cerebral view of reality which transcends time. It is obviously only on a superficial level that Swift is concerned with the Royal Society in Gulliver's journey to Laputa, that Dickens is con-

cerned with utilitarianism in *Hard Times,* that Fowles is concerned with semiology in *Mantissa.* The artist's human
understanding enfolds the critic's scientific model. The critic,
naturally, would like to reverse this relationship. *Mantissa* is the
novelist's counter-reversal: "I have a right to establish my own
non-connection at all in my own personal way" (II), Green complains, inadvertently deflating the theoretical balloon he has
been so anxious to inflate.

As pastiche ironically reflecting various stereotyped modes of
ultrainternalized and ultraexternalized fiction, *Mantissa* shapes
a highly ambiguous outline of the professional novelist. A
neurologist specializing in abnormal brain function, Dr. Delfie
tells Green (who has forgotten his social identity) that his profession "has an extremely long and well-recorded history of
general incapacity to face up to the realities of life" (I). Green is
of course a caricature to be admired for its lightness of touch,
its casual self-irony; yet at the same time there is a possibility of
glimpsing a subtle, ruthless, almost masochistic interior prob-
ing: the novelist's psychological X-ray photography of himself.
In this perspective *Mantissa* expresses, as an indirect elabora-
tion of the present foreword, an eternal preoccupation with the
complex nature of the writing self: the fears of imaginative
constipation, the quest for an escape from verbalization, for an
endlessly revisable "[t]ext without words" (IV).

Miles Green is the alienated and self-alienating bourgeois
artist whose swooning self-pity hardly deserves his creator's
compassion. He is, indeed, shown no mercy, for in his perverse
mental framework the extremes of self-effacement and narcissism are but the expressions of a single, monolithic self-
importance. Nevertheless Miles Green and John Fowles do
share, apart from the number of letters in their names, a common profession, a common ambiguity as makers of fiction and
creators of myth, and to keep them entirely separate is rather
difficult in the deliberate confusion of parody and self-parody,
author and character, text and nontext.

If the trend in the genre has been to write fiction about
writing fiction and to write fiction about the difficulty of writing
fiction, *Mantissa* would seem to carry this movement to its utter-
most extreme in being fiction about the impossibility of writing
fiction. Certainly failure is an important motif, for the narrative
structure is that of an endlessly interrupted nontext, a deliber-

ately unsuccessful sequence of coeternal revisions reflexively revising themselves: in nostalgic retrospect, in unfolding presentness, in creative and self-destructive anticipation of imminent nonbirth. "I'll feel different in a minute," says the reluctant muse. "When we start the next revision." But on this one-hundred-and-eighty-third page of *Mantissa* the novelist only sulks and complains: "I've had you just a miserable twice in what would have been, if this wasn't an unwritable non-text, one hundred and eighty-three pages at least" (IV).[25] Here the infinite number of possible erotic positions comes to mirror the infinite number of narrative alternatives, the terrifying freedom of an endless amount of authorial postures, of unreal stratagems, of verbal combinations that preexist on the unwritten page. Fowles focuses the difficulty of chosing a single path, a viable exist from the merry-go-round of a creative consciousness that perceives too many alternative routes, that anticipates an eerie host of potential revisions before having traced a tentative outline. Inside the chamber of creative consciousness, inside the gray walls of the mental hospital room where the novelist sustains his mute dialogue with himself, the ever-changing, ever-questioned boundary line between real and fictional identity is eternally blurred. In a matter of seconds, "in the tiny interstice of time between apogee and impact" (IV), the imaginative detail is transferred from the haze of immaterial thought in the novelist's dream to the distinct, discrete, and discontinuous linear reality of the typewritten sentence. Yet even in this magical metamorphosis nothing actually sensually tangible *takes place:* the written text remains unwritten, unmaterialized. All dialogue is interior, mute, all courage escape, all action consolation, all eroticism verbal. "You're doing exactly what you always do," the muse tells Green: "chasing your own tale" (*sic,* II). *Mantissa* is a blackhole in contemporary fiction: a centripetal acceleration of gravitation within the author's mind which carries the reader through the swirling funnel of an imagination so complex and swift in its flickering crosscurrents of associative thought that all threatens to be lost in a vortex of incomprehensible self-indulgence: the death-wish, perhaps, of the creative imagination, of a genre, of a species.

Metamorphosis is the literary transcendence of those taboos which camouflage the inherent ambiguity of our multilateral consciousness. The radical qualitative distinctions of mutually exclusive states of mind are unacceptable to a society and to a superego which, for the sake of stability, both insist on the illusion of oneness. All metamorphosis is therefore subversive terrorism, a guerrilla warfare of the bilateral against the unilateral, of the multiverse against the universe, of daily reincarnation against daily death, of the uncomfortable psychological pluralism of self-contradictory maturity against the secure psychological monism of the womb. The transition from innocence to experience takes shape, therefore, as a series of abrupt *reversals*.

Mantissa contains a dozen metamorphoses: (1) Dr. Delfie gives way to a punk girl; (2) the punk girl becomes Erato, the muse; (3) Miles Green becomes naked; (4) Erato once more becomes Dr. Delfie; (5) she becomes invisible; (6) the muse again materializes as neuropsychologist; (7) the gray walls (of the mind) dissolve during the erotic embrace of novelist and muse; (8) the gray walls immediately return to their state of impenetrable solidity; (9) Miles Green becomes a satyr; (10) Erato becomes a Japanese pleasure girl; (11) she vanishes for good; (12) the novelist returns to human form.

The formal structure of *Mantissa* is that of absurd reversal. This is chiefly expressed in the proportions between narrative and intrusion, and in the relationship between author and character. These features have been present in Fowles's previous fiction, but they have never been carried to such an outrageous extreme. We may recognize from *The French Lieutenant's Woman* the notion of a rebellious, self-willed character striving for autonomy vis-à-vis author: Charles's resentment toward the bearded man in the train compartment. Here Erato is totally dissatisfied with her author-parent Miles Green, accusing him first of modern authorial indifference in allowing the text to write its immoral self, and then, when he really gets going, of the old-fashioned male novelist's Machiavellian totalitarianism. She wants it both ways, and whatever Miles Green does, he always loses. "I'm in charge here," says Green (II) whose authorial omnipotence, provoked by the muse's moralistic teasing, suggests the absurdity of his lecture on the novelist's contemporary superfluity. In a dialogue of escalating vituperation novelist and character/muse accuse each other of breaking the rules. Erato has the nerve to profit from the gifts bestowed on her by the submissive novelist's magic, while at the same time resenting the power this gives him. At her command he produces out of thin air, by a snap of his fingers, an ashtray, a lighter, a cigarette box, and a pair of blue-tinted glasses whose chic frames carry the ironic trademark "Jane Austen" (II). "No trouble. Just another couple of lines" (II), says the smug novelist as he ingratiatingly offers the muse a cup of coffee; but only a while ago she has gone into one of her many tantrums: at her command Green demurely goes to switch off the white panel of light above the bed, but another panel, which has never been there before, is discovered glowing above the door, and over this the novelist has no power. Again Erato accuses Green of cheating: "'You've just invented that.' He raises his hands in denial. 'Oh yes you have. There hasn't been a single mention of it before this.'" (II).

Not only are the proportions in *Mantissa* between narrative and intrusion reversed, the bulk of the book consisting of an intrusion (sections 2–4); there is the additional reversal of agent: it is the polymorphic character who interrupts the novelist rather than a polyglottal narrative presence intruding upon the set actions of an individual protagonist. There is also present in *Mantissa* a strong suggestion of a further reversibility: a reversal of the fashionable reversal of the relationship between writer and text. By giving the character too much power and the writer almost none at all Fowles, paradoxically, achieves a reversion to traditionalist writing. The psychological mechanisms of this critical disappearing act are cunningly suggested as Miles Green tries to overcome his amnesia and recollect his original identity. This is the contemporary novelist's attempt to define and recover that creative autonomy which the deconstructivists would seem to deny him: "It occurred to him, with a dawning excitement, that this intuitive sense of what he could never have been might be a useful clue to what he actually was" (I). The not very farfetched extrapolation is that what we need is not so much further structuralist studies of the structure of the language of novelists to prove that the text writes the novelist, but structuralist studies of the structure of the language of structuralists and poststructuralists to prove that criticism writes the critic: that, not infrequently, we should perhaps consider the existence of an academic jargon that writes itself, mechanically and impersonally, the letters of the critic's name on the title page being rather superfluous footnotes, redundant mantissae. In giving this book its ironic title Fowles suggests both the essential triviality of the subgenre of fiction-fiction and the fundamental absurdity of considering a four-thousand-year-old tradition of literary creativity in parenthetical relationship to the transient phase of a nihilistic fad, a critical punk vogue.

In the free play of a nontext without ontological anchors the muse is obviously rather superfluous, and when she intrudes with a violent CRASH in the very last word of Part 1, she appears in the self-writing text as an alien ornithological phenomenon which, much like the cuckoo, turns up as an unpleasant migratory freak, a redundant mutation in the spring grove of crypto-Derridean warblers. Clearly the dehumanized, clinical pseudo-eroticism of Part 1 is for Fowles the pornography of the author-free text that writes itself. Under sedation, power cut, and anesthetic, Miles Green has no more conscious influence over the shaping of the text than a pregnant woman has over the formation of features in the growing fetus. All is passiveness in relation to the sound and fury of husband, midwife, and hazard. The manuscript is delivered to the semidrugged and surprised novelist as a baby is condescendingly shown to a woman who has given birth to a child without really knowing it. She is patronizingly praised by the maternity-ward staff, who believe that they themselves have done all the hard work, the real creative labor. Indeed Miles Green is quite confounded when he is persuaded to keep his genital rhythm for the sake of his *baby* (I), and when Nurse Cory has knocked and shuffled the papers together, she cradles them in her crooked right arm so as to proudly show him the infant:

> 'It's a lovely little story. And you made it all by yourself.'
> He stared uncomprehendingly at her inanely sentimental grin down at him. . . .
> 'Look, Mr. Green. Listen.' She bent her pretty capped head to read the top page, using a finger to trace the words, as she might have touched a newborn nose or tiny wrinkled lips. '"It was conscious of a luminous and infinite haze, as if it were floating, godlike, alpha and o-me-ga. . . ."' (I)

The reader recognizes the first lines of *Mantissa*, Part 1 being, like *Daniel Martin*, a fictional unit which begins where it ends, and in which novelist and narrator become entirely indistinguishable.

As nonauthor, Green resents having been awakened from

the nonexternal context of new hedonism, from the pornography of the text without determinate authorial intention; but as nascent creative author gradually becoming conscious of the text he begins to resent the new formalism which has carried the pleasure principle of Barthes's *jouissance* to its nauseating limit:

> if you had only manifested yourself earlier in the text to which you object so much . . . the narrative development you most particularly take exception to would almost certainly not have taken place and we should therefore not be respectively standing and kneeling here in this absurd hospital room that I haven't even had the patience to describe properly by square old standards (comma) let alone *nouveau roman* ones. . . . (II)

Sealed off from the contamination of extraneity, the nonwriter exists in the nonontological nonrealm of the deconstructivist's abyss, a masculine and formalistic world of supreme anonymity (Miles Green has to be told who he is) and dehumanization: "the fundamental preoccupation of the modern novel still unfortunately has to be mediated through various superficial masks and props, alias men and women" (II). In this male universe of total reification the determinancy of living human beings is a threat, as is the determinancy of those other mantissae, words: "With women one always ends in a bog of reality, alias words" (IV).

Green moves centrifugally from the decentered abyss of the nontext to the walls of his interiorized world: the cuckoo clock goes raving mad in a continuum of jeering exclamations as the frustrated novelist finally rockets like a kamikaze pilot into the iron curtain of his self-imposed incarceration. Erato, on the other hand, moves centripetally in the opposite direction, from physical extraneity to fictional interiorization. The muse, indeed, suggests "a reversal of normal narrative development" (II): instead of fictional situations growing out of real human relationships, some kind of casual *hors-texte* friendship in the real world might be contrived out of the "surrealistic preamble" (II). This would allow the book to externalize itself beyond its purely literary dimension into the sociological order of contemporary issues existing in quotidian time: nuclear disarmament, ecology, and so forth; she herself, meanwhile, would move inward into the more literary dimension and become, perhaps, "an associate editor with one of the literary magazines" (II).

In *Mantissa,* in fact, Fowles does not seem to concern himself so much with internalization itself as with the process of clinical severance, that bisection of consciousness which creates the absurdly monistic antipodes of elitism and vulgarism, ultrainteriorization and ultraexteriorization. Erato is exclusive when one considers "the point zero zero one percent of our hopeful readership who have even heard her name" (II). Yet counterbalancing this elitism stands her own stereotyped celebrations of a purely externalized reality in which all aspects of literary art must carry "a viable sociological function" (II). In a fictional world of literary extremes the "masculinity" of internalized fiction-fiction is matched in its degree of purification only by an opposite one-dimensionality: the supreme externality of the "women's novel."

Strangely, *Mantissa* is simultaneously Fowles's most physically alarming and most intellectually abstract work. Here he explores not only the myth of the signifier (text) as transparency, but also that of the autonomous signified ("truth," "reality"). The only alternative that Miles Green can see to the entirely autonomous and cerebral world of fictional introspection is the purely mimetic writing that exists in "a certain kind of women's novel these days" (II). The pornographic element in his own work he defends on the ground that it is, by contrast, completely cerebral: "Before you started interfering today the sexual component was absolutely clinical—if I may say so, rather cleverly deprived of all eroticism. . . . Clearly metaphysical in intent, at least to academic readers, who are the only ones who count nowadays" (II). What is frightening, here, is perhaps not Green's hypocrisy (cashing in on pornography while gaining a critical reputation as a highbrow man of letters), but his sincerity. Miles Green really does admire the "purely clinical," whether this is cerebral or physical. What he does not like is the integration of the two. This would create confusion. Physical reality, extraneity in general, is therefore something filthy but, alas, unavoidable; and so it becomes very convenient to treat it as a street girl, who will fulfill this base but insistent need while remaining in splendid, uncontaminating isolation. The erotic spatiotemporal dimension of existence is broken down into reified monads: sex, a ripening-shed for bananas, a cuckoo clock.

Miles Green looks twice, ten times the man of the world in his well-cut suit, his old school tie; not of course (these are the 1980s) in the least ashamed at having found time in a busy day to spend an hour or so with what is, after all, essentially a mere call-girl; but now going on, refreshed, to more serious matters—a meeting with his agent, perhaps, or a literary conference, or the blessedly masculine peace of his club. For the first time there is a sense of rightness in the room, of sane reality. (II)

Yet Fowles does not let Green get away with this convenient compartmentalization into exterior and interior, female and male, physical and metaphysical. Green's view is the perspective of the cerebral left showing everything beyond its own gray walls as mantissae. Therefore, as he marches confidently to that door, which a few pages later shows him only a reflection of himself, he finds there is no exit, only "an unbroken wall of grey quilting" (II). What is at stake here, in the sexual conflict between the nonauthor and the muse, would seem to be victory in the contest between the corporeality of discourse and its voice, its ideality of meaning. Ironically, this corporeality of the text, uncontaminated by authorial intentionality and inspiration, is the outcome of reification, of purely cerebral and internal operations, whereas the invisibility of the muse is a thing of radical incarnation. At one end of the spectrum we find "a completely abstract and unreal disputation. Essentially in the same category as the old scholastic one about the number of angels who can play hopscotch on a needle's point" (II). At the other extreme all is external: "Everything must be 'real', or it doesn't exist" (IV). Green travels from the comforts of amnesia to the painfulness of satyriasis, which for him is a fall "from true divinity and Descartes" (IV).

The hardcover grayness of the original Cape edition and the softcover grayness that lines the interior of Green's hospital room suggest the significance of the introductory quotations (preceding Parts 1 and 3) from Descartes's *Discours de la Méthode* (1637). By excluding extraneity ("I could pretend that I had no body, that no outer world existed") the French philosopher could define the essence of the human soul as something entirely noncorporeal. The senses, in this theory, are devoid of divinity. This Cartesian transection of human consciousness lays the foundation for three hundred years of cerebral lop-

sidedness in the name of "science." The neurological trouble
with Green, says Dr. Delfie, is that he has a "pathologically
hypertrophied right cerebral lobe" (III). Representing this
non-Cartesian dimension of consciousness, the muse views the
cerebral *left* with equal revulsion: "Has it never occurred to
your poor little male brain that logic, as you call it, is the mental
equivalent of the chastity belt?" (III).

It would be naïve to assume here that Fowles is championing
the right against the left, the female against the male, exterior
against interior, sensibility against sense. As in Doris Lessing's
The Marriages between Zones Three, Four, and Five (1980) sterility
(private, social, creative) follows the divorce between mutually
complementing aspects of consciousness and the ensuing bias.
For Erato the novelist's cerebral *jouissance* within the text does
not match the sensual equivalent in physical reality, which she
knows he despises: "I'm sure you'd much rather be having
some boring discussion about the parameters of contemporary
narrative structure" (II); for Green the muse's dedication to
external reality and spatiotemporal location is but "the tedious
monism of the real world outside the grey-quilted room" (IV).

Green's amnesia, his lack of real sensibility and real sensuality
(reflected in the pornographic preamble), is his disconnection
from the psychological right. This side of his bilateral consciousness must not be verbalized in the unilateral text, and in
his final reverie he imagines the whole female hemisphere con-
veniently reduced to a mute Japanese pleasure girl, "peerlessly
dumb—except perhaps for one or two hoarse and incomprehensible whimpers of discreetly grateful oriental pleasure . . . in
his right cerebral lobe" (IV). The Cartesian mind/body dualism, most clearly expressed in the *Traité des passions de l'âme*
(1649), marks a clear break with the classical notion of an inclusive mind which reflects the totality of experience; creating,
extending, interpreting, coloring, and transcending rather
than excluding, selecting, rejecting, dehumanizing, and estranging. To defend its unilateral logocentrism the Cartesian
mind *(l'âme forte)* must reject the ambiguity and complexity of
the multilateral, steer resolutely away from the unsettling
equivocation of the whole. Mistaking, in this perspective, the
transcendental for the regressive, the novelist rejects the muse,
and his punishment is one in which sexuality becomes a sublimation of writing rather than vice versa: "you are overattached
to the verbalization of feeling, instead of to the direct act of

feeling itself" (I) Dr. Delfie tells Miles Green. And so the novelist unwrites himself. Numbness becomes dumbness: the mute dialogue of uncontaminated flesh.

"We thought it added a human touch" (I), says the neuropsychologist in reference to the clock in the gray periphery of the novelist's mind. But the striking mechanism has been disconnected. In the subtemporal "seminar *à deux* on the subject of ourselves" (II) time is of marginal significance in spite of our knowledge that it always has the last word.

12 Occlusion

Any substance that rotates polarized light clockwise . . . is said to be dextrorotary. If it rotates the light counterclockwise it is levorotary. . . . Ordinary table sugar, for instance, or sucrose, rotates polarized light to the right. So does grape sugar, a form of glucose. Grape sugar is sometimes called dextrose because of its right-handedness. Fructose, or fruit sugar, on the other hand, rotates polarized light the other way and for that reason is often called levulose. . . . It was recently discovered that the difference in the smell of oranges and lemons is caused by differences between right and left forms of limonene.

Martin Gardner, *The Ambidextrous Universe*

The left hemisphere apparently plays the major role in "ordinary" temporal experiences by analysing events and temporal sequences of events. The right hemisphere apparently plays the major role in temporal experiences in some altered states of consciousness by synthesizing atemporal interconnections between events and enabling humans to experience the timelessness of existence. An understanding of both modes of temporal functioning seems to be an essential pre-requisite to an understanding of consciousness. . . . Differences in the functioning of the two cerebral hemispheres may underlie the linear and nonlinear constructions of time.
Richard A. Block, "Time and Consciousness" (in G. Underwood and R. Stevens, *Aspects of Consciousness*)

The structure of Fowles's imaginative universe (to use a rather outmoded but nevertheless perfectly valid term) is itself fascinating. Equally fascinating, however, are the wider implications of the Fowlesian paradigm. In this chapter I shall use my paradigm of human temporalities to define more precisely the structure of human time and the structure of consciousness. I will be using criticism to fuse fiction with psychobiology neuropsychology, neurosociology, neurolinguistics, and chronosophy (the study of time), much as Fowles, more recklessly, brings novelist into violent confrontation with neurologist and cuckoo clock in *Mantissa*. My interdisciplinary field here is that of *neuropoetics*—the study of the relationship between literature

144

and consciousness. To focus the Fowlesian spiral staircase from time to timelessness is to glimpse the DNA-molecule of consciousness, the cryptic choreography of the soul. The chromosomes of awareness are structured in the hologram of the mind so as to form a double helix in harmony with the vaster spirals of anticyclones and galaxies.

The various temporal moods and temporalities correspond, obviously, to fundamentally incompatible modes of consciousness alternating in comparative autonomy in daily life. Everyone knows that there is a difference between sleep and wakefulness. Most people also know that sleep can be subdivided into qualitatively different phases such as dream-sleep and nondream-sleep. To discriminate between the phases one only has to record the presence or absence of rapid eye movement. Similarly, there are profound qualitative discrepancies between modes of wakefulness, but only highly sensitive and introspective individuals care to consider the reality of such transitions, and those who have bothered to record them in all their phantom heterogeneity are easily numbered. I would like to suggest here, that just as rapid eye movement is a sure indication of a radical qualitative change within sleep, the altered apprehension of time is a sure indication of an altered state of wakefulness. And in such a context the idea that "out-of-time" experiences are manifestations of some form of regression is nonsense. The significance here of hemisphere research is that it has established the existence of *qualitatively different and often incompatible modes of consciousness.* What relationships there are between mode of awareness, cerebral lobe, cerebral dominance, handedness, hemisphere function and so forth, matters very little from our point of view. The important thing is that we know there *are* incompatible modes which cancel one another. Since Freud, literary criticism has been directly or indirectly preoccupied with the subdivisions of consciousness known as id, ego, and superego. Indeed Fowles often thinks consciously along such lines, and in *The Aristos* he adds to these concepts the notion of the *nemo.* This suggests dissatisfaction with the rather outmoded Freudian categories. In fact John Fowles has an extraliterary interest in a number of things, and it is this Renaissance all-roundness of the man which makes him more than an ordinary novelist, his novels more than ordinary novels. This analytical Frenchness of Fowles, expressed in his liking for the *roman à thèse,* in his arrogant literary sermonizing,

explains some of his alienation from the fundamental Englishness of a literary establishment which abhors discursive
and didactic intrusions.

The principal weakness, I think, of the Freudian model is
that it subdivides consciousness into *horizontal* layers so as to
form a hierarchy; hemisphere research, on the other hand,
establishes the existence of two cerebral lobes which function as
parallel computers. A popular misrepresentation of the theory
suggests that consciousness itself is compartmentalized into the
lobes, so that one thinks logically with the left and intuitively
with the right; it is more meaningful to speak of qualitative
individual differences in the *degree of lateralization,* the point
being that certain individuals have an altogether different flexibility and integration of neuronal structures. There seems to be
a significant correlation with handedness, creativity, and vul-
nerability (mental as well as physical).[26] Typically left-handed or
mixed-handed diffusion reflects a fundamentally holistic way
of perceiving reality in complex three-dimensional visual and
aural "molecules" of thought-feelings; right-handed and more
distinct lateralization, on the other hand, expresses itself in
discrete "atoms" of serialized data on the conveyor belt of
time.[27]

It is now possible to buy an expensive digital-type wristwatch,
which with a flick of a finger can be *reversed* so as to become a
dial-type watch; a different kind of watch will show *simultaneously* a dial face and a digital face. In the novels, we may think
of Fowles as alternating between the masks of time, occasionally
flicking the first watch into a complicated *sequence of reversals,* at
other times displaying the second type of watch: the *superimposed layers* of a holographic and linear temporality in double
exposure.

In musical and pictorial art the aural and visual "molecules"
do not have to pass through the two-dimensional quarantine of
verbalization. Superficially, this is an advantage. At further
consideration it is a disadvantage, for the linear right-
handedness of the printed word forces the right to establish a
rapport with the left. Words do not relate themselves to the
novelist's vision as the printed notes of music relate themselves
to the composer's symphony, for whereas it would be possible
for a musical genius to arrange his symphony without the support of printed notes, the novelist *is* the printed word—its

muteness. In this context Fowles's concern for *not* reading from his novels is significant.

The writing of fiction, therefore, is a supremely translateral form of activity, necessarily involving incompatible modes of temporality. What would an individual do in order to express the *total* experience of his life? Writing poetry, or painting, or composing music would be to linger too much in the free nebulous world of a blurred cognitive style without the sculptured distinctness of critical thought; performing laboratory experiments and writing scientific essays would be to deny oneself the freedom of including the full power of imaginative self-assertion and right to impose value-judgements. To write novels would bring one close to the absolute meridian, slightly to the right. To arrive smack on target and hover above the cerebral meridian, much as certain satellites maneuver so as to hover permanently above the equator, a little navigation to the left remains to be done: the novelist makes small extratextual excursions; writes, perhaps, an essay on his novel, or on his protagonist, or on himself, or on the business of writing. And to make absolutely sure that his navigation actually succeeds, he takes pains to make such excursions integrative segments of the creative self. Thus the novelist gives way freely to a sinistral bias so as to become, in his novels about writing novels, a literary critic. In wishing to achieve the full zenith that overlooks in equidistant completeness the entire interfused territory in between the extreme poles of sinister atomization and dextral holism, the imaginative critic will of course move in the opposite direction, away from the hinterland of pedestrian technicians. And so the critic transcending criticism and the novelist transcending the novel meet and become indistinguishable in the *Corpus callosum* of a supremely integrated reality. In the achieved hologram lateralization is so weak and flexibility so extreme that novelist and critic can change places in a reversal of identities analogous to the contralateral manner in which the right brain controls left hand and left brain right hand. *Mantissa*, in fact, is to a very high degree a work of literary criticism. Fowles has become critic, while the pseudocritic's role of passive reviewer is taken over by the novelist (Miles Green).

The neurologist's dilemma is that, having completed his experiment and left the laboratory, he falls in love with his new assistant over a cup of coffee, or sees a child run over by a lorry on the way home from work, or notices some subtle change in the amethyst twilight, sending his total being into a violet reverie so fleeting, faint, and aerial in its distilled essence that it passes almost without conscious recognition. Slowly it sinks down with other iridescent dregs of the extraprofessional quotidian to form a kind of accumulated sediment. Only in sentimental retrospect can this be perceived as a globular transparency, a decorative, domestic pendant to the nonprivate and objective world of research.

Now the novelist is inclusive, not exclusive. His laboratory is the cosmos; his experiment life itself. For him *any* exclusion is treason, as Fowles declares confidently in the first/last sentence of *Daniel Martin:* "Whole sight; or all the rest is desolation." Whatever sediment he finds must be stirred and shaken into new time-spot spirals in the manner of a child snowflaking the water-encapsuled dreamworld of a Christmas toy. The neurologist might want to condense his extraprofessional dream into an amateur sonnet kept on some secret shelf behind a heavy camouflage of scientific magazines; but there is no way in which he can *directly* transmit his subjective experience into the project, for the thought-feelings of his daydream occur outside the controlled conditions of the laboratory. For the novelist *all* conditions are controlled. In writing there is no time out.

A well-known metaphor suggesting the nature of cerebral dominance is one describing the right intellect as that of stars and the left intellect as that of the sun. When the sun shines perception of the stars vanishes. Yet the stars are still there. They are blotted out, not by something more beautiful, but by something more powerful. Since the left hemisphere is that in which the awareness of a linear temporality predominates, *this sun is time* from our perspective. The experience of being removed out of time is the experience of seeing the whole starlit heaven, as the blinding light of the totalitarian sun suddenly vanishes. Henceforth I will be referring to the sinistral as *solar* and to the dextral, or ambidextral, as *astral.* I shall refer to the temporality of the nonsinistral as *holotemporality* or *dextrotemporality* and to that of the sinistral as *levotemporality.*[28] I am not suggesting a simple left-right switch in the brain, but a sudden transfer from the psychological left to the psychological right. *Some* sort of radical shift of power does take place in the brain. It will be appreciated how wonderfully accurate Fowles is in his perception, description, and creation of such violent transitions in our consciousness. Fowles's self-observations also tally in a very striking manner with the neurological hypothesis that *something vanishes*. The structuring of reality that we associate with the psychological left must release its hold if that other and far more exhilarating structuring of reality is to come into existence: "time" must disappear. I think the sudden illumination of the night-sky of consciousness is the most intense of all human experiences, stronger, in fact, than the purely physical orgasm. I think therefore also that the driving force involved is the strongest and most ruthless on our planet. The success of Fowles's writing can to a large extent be seen in the light of this ability to produce in the reader exactly those convulsive shudders, or temporality-switches, that constitute the orgasms of consciousness. The perfect balance of frequency is that of *The French Lieutenant's Woman*. It is also very clear to me that what the religious or mystic calls "salvation", "revelation", or "initiation" is nothing other than a first intense and conscious experience of the vanishing of serial time. When the time-sun sets on the consciousness of the mature mind the shock of the release from the two-dimensionality of the left to the three-dimensionality of the right is so shattering that the mind will form an unconditional and lifelong attachment to whatever medium is present. In all cases the sworn allegiance will be "eternal" and carried out with fanatical determination and little consideration for common-sense appreciations of the ambivalence of personality or dogma. What worth the left attaches to the adored person or creed matters little, for the "right" has taken its height in one flash of crystalline knowledge. The problem here, of course, is that sailing the night-seas of human experience the wandering bark of consciousness thinks it has measured the infinite height of the medium, whereas in actual fact it has measured its own height. The medium, as Charles Smithson discovers with Sarah Woodruff, belongs both to the sunlit and starlit hemispheres; it is not very surprising, therefore, that madonna becomes whore for the man who expects a bilateral human being to offer a monolateral release from the irresolvable conflicts of the human condition. This irresolvability of the conflicts of the mind expresses the incompatibility of left and right thinking.

The fiction of John Fowles reveals how the three-dimensional constellation of the dextral only come into full play

when the two-dimensional stream of the sinistral is somehow
ousted from its usual role as totalitarian *Roi Soleil.* The sinistral
intellect achieves its "control" and fake supremacy through a
dramatic narrowing of consciousness and a violent dissociation
of sensibility. Yet on the highest levels of the mental hierarchy
of man the most subtle, sophisticated, and complex cognitive
mechanisms are based on interpenetrations, bisociations, and
cross-fertilizations within the largest possible associative con-
texts of the mind. In the mutilated adult consciousness reared
on the temporal diet of technomonetary levotemporality the
sudden orgastic access to holotemporality *adds a new and higher
level* to the mental and temporal hierarchy. Science never really
has access to this highest integrative level of consciousness, for,
as Fowles points out in *The Aristos* (9/42), the achievement of
pure "objectivity" in scientific research requires a kind of cognitive puritanism that isolates a chaste mental *sub*mechanism.
In reference to the highest integrative levels of consciousness,
which are supremely *inclusive* rather than supremely *exclusive,*
this "scientific" reliability, artificially created by narrowing
down the mind of man to a slender strip of "logic," becomes
clinical sterility, frigidity, impotence. Viewed from the apex of
full human awareness, "objectivity" is objectification. A ray of
light is pretty colorless and neutral in comparison with the
seven prismatic colors that it can be broken *down* into. Similarly,
the brilliance of great writing and art is almost invisible when
examined with eyes accustomed to the spectacular and colorful
definitions that the scientist makes as he climbs down to a lower,
less integrated, more "lateralized," level of human awareness.
The Fowles novel is a prism first breaking the dextrotemporal
invisibility of the "timeless" into levotemporal rainbows; then
reversing that right–left stream from timelessness to time into
the left–right channels of the printed page. Beyond the colored
time-patterns of that finite print trapped in the luminosity of
time, there is always an invisible text, eternally writing itself in a
colorless now, knowing, in spite of external change, that it is all
colors, pasts, futures.

Significantly, the Fowlesian protagonist countermanipulates
the manipulations of two-dimensional temporality by muffling
the solar din of madding crowds. In the solitude of a sacred
combe removed from sinistral temporality the stellar magic of
dextrotemporality acquires an uninterrupted hold on the
imagination. This retreat is really conquest, for it is of course

that from which retreat has been made that is the real retreat: pornoland, discoland, computerland, newsland, dollarland, missileland, fashionland, medialand, gossipland, theoryland, videoland . . . *thing*land. This is the retreat of the multilateral from the unilateral, and the innumerable retreats in literary history, from Swift to Rousseau, are only superficially geographical and socio-political. Isolated in a Sussex cottage, Syrian desert, Dorset wood, or Greek island, the Fowlesian protagonist is released from levotemporality. He now begins to notice the restricted two-dimensionality, limited validity, and flatness of the jigsaw puzzle of his past. As the emerging stellar molecules suggest an additional dimension in the geometry of consciousness, the protagonist begins to dismantle his flat past into its constituent time-fragments so as to be able to reassemble them into a valid and rounded totality.

What I find so exciting here is that the conceptual differences between the protagonist's initial, flat identity and subsequently reassembled identity are stunning parallels to the conceptual differences that leading neurologists believe exist between the cerebral organization of the typical right- and left-hander. Graham Beaumont uses the following analogies to contrast the more clearly lateralized sinistral intellect of the right-hander (bear in mind that left hand mirrors right lobe) with the greater diffusion and higher degree of integration in the dextral system of the typical nonright-hander. The sensitive reader will no doubt appreciate the ample relevance of the following metaphor with respect to qualitative changes in the Fowlesian protagonist (especially in *Daniel Martin*), to lines of argument in Fowles's foreword, and indeed to the general structure of this present interdisciplinary chapter:

> The brain of the right hander is seen as rather like a campus in which books and journals are kept in departmental libraries. These libraries are connected by well organised pathways, but are nevertheless some distance apart. The brain of the non-right hander is more like a campus which has one large central library in which all books and journals are stored, and which has a cataloguing system which makes even relatively related subjects somewhat diverse within the confines of the library building.
> The simple task is, therefore, like a researcher inspecting the material relating to a simple and well defined topic, easily contained within the scope of a single discipline. For this

work, the advantage will lie in the first campus, where the researcher can sit in the small departmental library which relates to his topic and have all the material almost within his reach. For complex, interdisciplinary research, however, the situation is reversed. The central library here will involve the researcher in little additional effort in the collection of material than was involved in the simple task.

In simple terms, the diffuse system, that of the left hander, carries an advantage for complex integrative operations, but a disadvantage for rapid simple communications.

An alternative analogy might be the relative organisation of transport systems. If in two countries, one concentrates its resources into great intercity highways, while the other develops a comprehensive network of first class trunk roads, which are by comparison relatively diffuse, then the first system will carry an advantage for the businessman travelling from one commercial center to another, while the second will be more suited to the agricultural chemist travelling around rural areas taking samples from scattered farms. The businessman is the simple task, the agricultural expert the more complex.[29]

It is of course far beyond my competence, and obviously not my intention, to attempt to clarify in any way the degree and nature of the correlations between handedness, hemisphere function, and creativity. What I am emphasizing is the general relevance of this neuropoetic perspective in comparison with "psychoanalytical" and crypto-Freudian modes of approach. Whereas the psychobiological right of the typical left-hander from a neuropsychological point of view amounts to a *parallel* form of conceptual organization, perhaps even an evolutionary variant (a dazzling speculation), it is from a conventional, Freudian perspective rather suspect, rather sinister. In the study of human time we must begin to appreciate the danger and mistake of viewing dextrotemporality as existing below the "normal" experience of quotidian time. The dextrotemporal is only abnormal or subnormal from the point of view of the levotemporal—from the point of view of scientific paradigms based on the sinistral ethos. Seen from the perspective of the dextral or ambidextral, levotemporality is equally restricted, regressive, atavistic, inane, foggy . . . immoral. I think it is the opalescence of dextrotemporality, produced by the greater diffusion of the more fully integrated consciousness, which leads the left to view the right as blurred, hazy, and indistinct. I also think the impression of this opaqueness is established only in retrospect, when the conscious mind has returned from the dextrotemporal. It is the dividing line between the two which is semi-impermeable. In fact the limpidity and translucence of the dextrotemporal is one of its most conspicuous features, a dextral counterpart of the analytical, causal clarity of the sinistral. The two temporalities are like parallel aquariums, one round, one rectangular, offering perfect intramural, but blurred transmural, visibility. The round aquarium to the right is filled with water "quivering within the wave's intenser day," as Shelley writes when defining aqueous color enhancement in his "Ode to the West Wind"; the oblong glass box to the left contains the equal but different clarity of air.

I have demonstrated through the fictional externalizations of Fowles's self-observations that "time" (levotemporality) and "timelessness" (dextrotemporality) are mutually beneficient. Yet in a strange way "timelessness" enfolds "time," while the reverse is an impossibility. This tallies very well with theories concerning the reductionism of the sinistral and the holism of the nonsinistral. An improvement of the aquarium imagery would therefore be a conception of the round bowl as a huge crystalline liquid sphere *containing* the sinistral air-box of time. We see this phenomenon illustrated in Fowles's observation that, through the levotemporal progression of an oboe, harpsichord, or piano, the protagonist continues to be aware of serial time *within* dextrotemporal (holotemporal) transcendence of that temporality. When Charles slips out of sinistral time into dextrotemporality with Lalage at the end of *The French Lieutenant's Woman,* he continues to be aware of two-dimensional, linear time within the three-dimensionality of his "out-of-time" experience: in the distant glass-house of time, now a faintly perceived musicbox, the jerky progression of a Chopin mazurka still makes itself felt. Time is still there, only now it is perceived in its infinite insignificance in relation to the entire globular hologram of dextrotemporality. This temporal West Berlin, this bubble of time within timelessness, of levotemporality within holotemporality, I call *planetary time:* the solar dwarfed and deflected so as to blend with the stellar.

"Out-of-time" experiences are said to involve a dissolution and transcendence of self and time. Yet this "self" and this "time" are merely the self and time of the sinistral. It is the sinistral language of levotemporal totalitarianism that uses these expressions so as to verbalize an experience which for the whole is not transcendence but recognition, restoration, realization. How foolish to think one is *out* of something in a piano concerto or a love affair!

The manic depression of novelists, mentioned in Fowles's foreword, also fits in very well here. For having existed so long in dextrotemporality as to develop gills, the novelist gasps for oxygen in the air-box of a sinistral reality, where there are no more living goldfish, not even an odd stickleback. Survival becomes amphibious adaptation.

As to the capacity of the integrated mind to perceive rounded, spiral molecules where others only see two-dimensional zigzags, there is also a negative aspect: a paranoiac tendency to see webs of relationships where there are none. The Fowlesian protagonist's world is one of supreme conspiracy: Miranda a victim of the New People conspiracy represented by Clegg; Charles a victim of the Victorian conspiracy led by Mr. Freeman and Mrs. Poulteney, and of the female conspiracy led by Sarah; Miles Green a victim of the conspiracy of the text led by the muse, and of that of erotic manipulation led by Dr. Delfie; Nicholas a victim of the conspiracy of the metatheater led by Conchis, and of that of sexual maliciousness led by Julie/Lily; Daniel Martin a victim of the conspiracy of Englishness led by Jane, of the tyrannical now led by Jenny, and of the tyrannical past led by his alter ego.

I have spoken of the disappearance of the time-sun as a shuddering orgasm of the mind, an Elizabethan "dying" which is precisely a dying of levotemporality. But just as there are many sexually frigid individuals who have never experienced erotic transcendence, who have never died a sensual death, so I believe there are many people, especially in our sinistral society, who are eternally alienated from dextrotemporal ecstasy. Any ideologically, erotically, or spiritually "saved" or "emancipated" reader who has tried to convey the quality of any such "salvation" to one not emancipated will appreciate the utter uselessness of words, of sinistral means of expression: a recurring Fowlesian motif. Neurologists believe that cerebral specialization varies widely not only between functions, but also between individuals.[30] There is nothing strange, therefore, in the notion that a tremendous number of people find all the talk about transtemporal experiences to be part of some esoteric conspiracy, some pseudoscientific and highly immoral cult which must be contemptuously dismissed or ruthlessly exterminated. The sinistral is awed by the three-dimensionality of the holotemporal, because this is sure proof of its own frigidity, inadequacy, and limited usefulness. In literature this is often reflected in the inability of the critic to work out valid scientific diagrams that come to terms with the artist's creative holograms: hundreds of pages of sinistral deconstruction, is required to transcribe from three-dimensionality to two-dimensionality what can be stated within dextrotemporality in fourteen lines. Fowles's *Mantissa*, I think, is a reaction against this desire of frigid two-dimensionality to discount the existence of an extrasinistral, non-Cartesian dimension.

We may recall from *The French Lieutenant's Woman* Mrs. Poulteney's Victorian worship of hard work, which is of course part and parcel also of the post-Victorian ethos. The monotonous drudgery glorified by the Puritan ethos has precisely the function of purifying consciousness from dextrotemporality: such noncreative labor dulls the astral senses and sharpens the sense of reality as an endless sequence of hours and minutes. Hard work reinforces lateralization and brings out that shallow sunshine world of middle-ground contentedness which protects the mind from its own latent "immorality," its sensitivity and Gestalt perception, or ability to see whole patterns.

As to Fowles's preoccupation with *the few*, this must ultimately also be seen in its basic neuropoetic context. The nonuniversality of those dextrotemporal epiphanies which permit the stars of a time-deserted, multimodal hologram to emerge out of the eclipsed blankness of the solar mind, creates a neuronal class conflict: the division of mankind into a nonorgastic solar proletariat and a postorgastic astral nobility. Between Heraclitus's *moral* few/many dualism and the Romano-Marxian *economic* patrician/plebeian dualism lies the *neuropsychological* right/left or astral/solar dualism which has turned up earlier in the West as the *religious, mystic,* and *esoteric* dualisms of eternally saved/eternally damned: the Calvinist and Jansenist preoccupation with divine grace and original sin. Another Western expression of the attempt to eternalize the shattering effect of the *Aurora Borealis* of consciousness is of course *amour courtois* and Celtic myth. As opposed to the solar pursuit of the manipulative paroxysms of coital conquest, the orgastic quest envisioned in this body of legends suggests a surrender to astral femininity: the myth of the Knights of the *Round* Table (pursuers of holistic understanding) and their attempts to perceive the invisible globular hologram of the Holy Grail. No image of the removal of levotemporal tyranny could be clearer than that of Arthur's drawing of the cemented sword, a feat most men were incapable of.

In *The Aristos* Fowles discusses the limited value of viewing games and sport in Freudian terms of sexual sublimation (9/65). In such a light the Arthurian sword and chalice would be phallic and vaginal symbols. I share the view that such interpretations are silly—revealing the shallowness of contemporary humanism and a gross underestimation of the length and depth of esoteric tradition, of the complexity of pretechnological culture. One of the outstanding features of Fowles's fiction is his ability to distinguish between the orgastic and the orgiastic; between the authentic achievement of cerebral shift and the corresponding imitative pseudovariant which resorts to artificial forms of intoxication. As Dionysian dextrotemporality becomes increasingly parenthetical within an ultra-Apollonian technocracy, the pleasure principle of a false hedonism becomes ever more hectic and frantic: the instant profit of the business present turns for the now generation into the instant ejaculation of a creature present.

For the quotidian time of levotemporality to fall away from the consciousness of Western man churned to pulp in the non-stop clockwork of industrialism, some sort of crisis is required—a crisis which removes most of the sense impressions of the merry-go-round. A surprising number of individuals are capable, just like Conchis, of specifying the exact spatiotemporal location of their astral orgasm, to pinpoint with minute accuracy the time-space spot of their "salvation," "initiation," or whatever they want to call it. For Arthur Koestler this experience occurred while he was awaiting execution in cell no. 40 of the Central Prison of Seville during the Spanish Civil War. Kept in solitary confinement from February 13 to May 14, 1937, Koestler refused any form of sentimental deathbed conversion to religiosity. Yet the change of conceptual organization forced upon him by solitude and sensory deprivation did finally trigger a permanent change of personality. The passage below is of great interest, for it suggests precisely (although in tentative metaphor) the triple-tiered paradigm of a multileveled hologram of temporalities outlined in this present study (chapter 10). One notices, here, the emphasis on the intellectual limpidity of the experience, on its nonmystic quality (in line with the Egyptologist's sobriety in *Daniel Martin*), and also the manner in which a switch to a previously unused mode of cerebral organization is described as the experiencing of a "higher order of reality." The transition to a different pattern of cerebral dominance is accompanied also, I am convinced, by a totally different mode of apprehending the inanimate. The reversed relative importance of the human and nonhuman with which Dickens was so preoccupied is no doubt an expression of a psychedelic magnification of reality which in the artist is quite commonplace and quotidian, but which in the average individual in our society can usually only be produced by extreme forms of manipulations from without: LSD, hypnotism, and so forth. In its natural form the experience has only positive aftereffects:

> Yet, "mystical" experiences, as we dubiously call them, are not nebulous, vague or maudlin. . . . When I say "the I had ceased to exist," I refer to a concrete experience that is verbally as incommunicable as the feeling aroused by a piano concerto, yet just as real—only much more real. In fact, its primary mark is the sensation that this state is more real than any other one has experienced before. . . .
> I was thus waging a two-front war against the concise, rational, materialistic way of thinking which, in thirty-two years of training in mental cleanliness, had become a habit. . . .
> The "hours by the window" . . . had filled me with a direct certainty that a higher order of reality existed, and that it alone invested existence with meaning. I came to call it later on "the reality of the third order." The narrow world of sensory perception constituted the first order; this perceptual world was enveloped by the conceptual world which contained phenomena not directly perceivable, such as gravitation, electromagnetic fields, and curved space. . . . Just as the conceptual order showed up the illusions and distortions of the senses, so the "third order" disclosed that time, space and causality . . . were merely optical illusions on the next higher level. . . . It was a text written in invisible ink; and though one could not read it, the knowledge that it existed was sufficient to alter the texture of one's existence, and make one's actions conform to the text.[31]

Can the incredible complexity of the human brain really function along the lines of such a simple dualism as that suggested by this theory of levotemporal/dextrotemporal conflict?

Undoubtedly. Consider weather, for instance. Every time you look out of the window there is a newborn set of atmospheric conditions which atom for atom is entirely unique. Yet it is possible to comprehend an underlying two-way system of cold and warm air masses. The Norwegian discovery of this in our century is still behind the forecasts now based on computer calculations and satellite pictures. The artist does not have to break down reality quite as ruthlessly as the scientist. In painting clouds Constable found it useful to categorize ten basic forms of cloud structures, just as we have already broken down the Fowlesian light beam into a spectrum of temporalities. Yet we must go further. We must define the cyclones and anticyclones of time, in order to determine the universal laws of human temporality.

All weather conditions are formed by the interaction between opposed air masses: warm air versus cold air. This conceptual simplification allows us to get away from a previous simple-mindedness: that of holding out a hand inside a warm front and saying: "Hallo, this is rain;" and then holding out a hand inside a cold front, saying: "Hallo, this is rain too!" This is analogous with the student of time and consciousness who, emptying a bottle of whisky, says: "Hallo, I'm passing out of time"; and then, twenty-four hours later attending a piano concerto: "Hallo, I'm passing out of time now too!" This type of reasoning in science produces a fatal fallacy in which the rainbows of consciousness are labeled slips from intelligence, when they in fact constitute the supreme achievements of intelligence. Again it is the Freudian model of the superimposed horizontal layers of the mind's ionosphere, stratosphere, etc., which creates the illusion that transitions must be ascents of descents, when they are really the products of interlocking spirals in a three-dimensional consciousness involving the lateralization of hemispheres.

You will never be able to understand time, consciousness, or yourself as long as you go on confusing warm fronts with cold fronts, descendental timelessness with transcendental timelessness. They have in common the orgasms of precipitation, but in most other respects they are structural opposites: the warm front is characteristically preceded by a high veil of cirrus, while the accompaniment of thunder belongs exclusively to the cold front, a detail overlooked by Fowles in *The French Lieutenant's Woman:* "The morning's azure sky was overcast by a high veil of cirrus, harbinger of that thunderstorm we have already heard in Lyme, and his mind soon began to plummet into a similar climate of morose introspection" (26). Dealing with the trade winds and turbulence of fiction rather than with those of real weather, Fowles can allow himself such meteorological peccadilloes. Yet in tracing the isobars and depressions of time he never makes the tiniest slip, and it is this which permits him to chart so miraculously the ridges and troughs of human consciousness.

In the centripetal eye of the hurricane of awareness the *counterclockwise* anticyclone of human experience is that of a wind lashing first in one direction, then, after a deceptive interlude, in the opposite. Timelessness is a whole, not a hole; a double helix, not a descending ladder. Time does not die into timelessness: it is born into timelessness. In fact time *feeds* on timelessness, and we all know instinctively the stupidity of languishing in his slow-chapped power. Like the Caribbean hurricane the time-timelessness spiral feeds on the heat it generates through its own process.

External weather is generated by differences in temperature; internal weather by differences in tension. The warm air mass of weather is that of humidity and heat; the cold air mass is that of dryness and coolness. The warm air mass of consciousness is that of dextrotemporal tensionlessness; the cold air mass of consciousness is that of levotemporal tension. In the Mid Atlantic of experience, where the anticyclones of temporality are born which sweep the vast continent of the mind, the warmer tropical air and the cooler polar air coexist peacefully along an invisible aerial curtain—much as the two modes of human awareness coexist fairly autonomously on each side of the iron curtain dividing the right and left of the clearly lateralized mind. Sooner or later some factor of instability will produce a wave on the previously taut membrane. Lateralization is weakened as in the case of indeterminate cerebral dominance. In the ensuing ambivalence and instability the peaceful border-line becomes a meandering front line as the red egalitarians of tensionlessness invade enemy territory in perfect synchronization with a corresponding lateral invasion by the blue nonegalitarians of competitive tension. Thus a whole chain of temporality-spirals is born out of the mid-sea of consciousness, gathering power progressively only to lose all energy in a cascade of condensation—a hopeless confrontation with the adamant resistance in the mountain ranges of an inflexible reality: a Sarah, a fossil . . . a muse aiming at the novelist with the twin-barreled rifle of punk and neurology.

Finally, in coming to grips with Fowles's recent attempt to state the self, whether writing or nonwriting, whether in *Daniel Martin* or *Mantissa,* we must consider the nature and structure of this dual self; the dichotomy of its conceptual organization.

"Out-of-time" experiences have in common that sensation of a dissolution of self which Freud labeled "oceanic," and which in the archaeology of sinistral knowledge has ever since been confined to the ghettos of mysticism and charlatanism. Dextrotemporality is supremely real, but not *in* the real (*dans le vrai* as Michel Foucault puts it); not in the real of the sinistral. Even in Fowles's extrafictional discourse the caution of its skepticism and sobriety is remarkable in relation to the lucidities of its collateral extravagances. The consternation of the left is conspicuous; its recognition of having recently experienced a heightened intelligence, a yet more transparent clarity, a yet more real reality; and at the same time the presence of a disbelieving faculty insisting on the monsterhood, anarchy, and madness of the alien.

It is very clear that in out-of-time experiences there is no dissolution of self at all, only a lateral transfer of self, a redistribution of power among competing selves. The alleged unpossessive altruism of the right is one big myth, though not a conscious fraud. The sweet thrill of ceasing to be a collector, of abandoning the will to power of the sinistral ego, would never be made into a philosophy of life without the compensatory emergence of another and far more intense self which cherishes much more precious possessions, territories, orgasms. It knows very well that it is getting the top cream of life in every living second. This is why the Battle of Britain was won, not lost. For when really threatened, the subtle, but hidden, self-assertion of the double mind goes berserk, revealing its essential arrogance and determination to retain its unique treasures. This is the elusive psychobiological paradigm of British history, and in defining the integrative complexities of Englishness, John Fowles has done a service to his country only equalled, in my opinion, by John Cowper Powys's writing of *Mortal Strife* (1942). In fact a better word than dextrotemporality to cover the sly self-protective consciousness of the integrated mind would be *anglotemporality,* by which I do not mean insular time but imperial time. The temporal tapestry of civilization defies the conveyor belt of objectified time, looks upon it as madness; the text is more than itself, not only because the present is more than itself, but also because the self is more than itself.

Notes

1. "Psychobiological Implications of Bilateral Asymmetry" in S. J. Dimond and J. G. Beaumont, eds., *Hemisphere Function in the Human Brain* (London: Elek, 1974), p. 167.

2. Stan Gooch, "Right Brain, Left Brain" (11 September 1980), pp. 790–92.

3. Norman Geschwind and Peter Behan, "Left-Handedness: Association with Immune Disease, Migraine, and Developmental Learning Disorder," *Proceedings of the National Academy of Science*, 79 (August 1982), 5097–100.

4. I have found a curious and striking parallel between the dualistic view of consciousness (see chapter 12) that I have worked out from Fowles's treatment of human time and the psychological dichotomy outlined by Arthur Koestler as the conflict between the *trivial* and the *tragic* in *The Act of Creation* (London: Hutchinson, 1964), ch. 20. Here Koestler also discusses humor at length. Humor and taboo, in my view, are mere safety devices which function so as to keep the cognitive repertoires apart and ensure sanity. When the two cognitive styles interpenetrate we laugh *because we "know" that this fusion is impossible*. Objects and events become stage props belonging to two different theaters of the mind. They are separated by taboo and fused, very briefly, by humor. In his novels Fowles breaks such taboos. These are essentially universal and psychological, not social or historical.

5. *The Integrated Mind* (New York: Plenum Press, 1978), pp. 159–61.

6. "Cognitive introspective psychology and related cognitive science can no longer be ingored experimentally, or written off as 'a science of epiphenomena' or as something that must in principle reduce eventually to neurophysiology. The events of inner experience, as emergent properties of brain processes, become themselves explanatory causal constructs in their own right, interacting at their own level with their own laws and dynamics. The whole world of inner experience (the world of the humanities), long rejected by 20th-century scientific materialism, thus becomes recognized and included within the domain of science." Roger Sperry, "Some Effects of Disconnecting the Cerebral Hemispheres," *Science* 217 (24 September 1982), 1226.

7. See Michael Corballis and Ivan L. Beale, *The Psychology of Left and Right* (Hillsdale, New Jersey: Lawrence Erlbaum Associates, 1976), pp. 177–83. Mixed-handers tend to have a very high or very low I.Q.

8. This is Jerre Levy's line of argument in S. J. Dimond and J. G. Beaumont, eds., *Hemisphere Function in the Human Brain* (London: Elek, 1974).

9. Handedness can obviously tell us nothing at all about the cerebral dominance of the individual player. The very high percentage of left-handers in the game, however, has raised questions for the psychologists with regard to the relationship between handedness, creativity, genius, originality, and verbalization. At the beginning of the final section of *Mantissa* Fowles uses one of his many game analogies as the rallies of discourse are merged with the nonverbal dialogue of the tennis court. There are hardly

any hidden pockets of latent meaning in the muse's comments on the novelist's "backhand smash," yet in the nontext of athletic poetry at its best it is not difficult to perceive the same processes of mental and verbal gearing that the human mind externalizes in the more respectable world of literature.

10. The right brain does seem to have a certain sense of time: "The nonvocal hemisphere appears to be cognizant of the person's daily and weekly schedules, the calendar, seasons, and important dates of the year." Yet the verbal/nonverbal dualism is a real feature of consciousness that we know more about today through hemisphere research: "Regardless of remaining uncertainties concerning laterality, one beneficial outcome that appears to hold up is an enhanced awareness, in education and elsewhere, of the important role of nonverbal components and forms of intellect." Roger Sperry, "Some Effects of Disconnecting the Cerebral Hemispheres," *Science* 217 (24 September 1982), 1225.

11. See J. T. Fraser *Of Time, Passion, and Knowledge* (New York: George Braziller, 1975), pp. 436–40.

12. See K. G. Denbigh, *An Inventive Universe* (London: Hutchinson, 1975), pp. 98 ff.

13. The same conflict turns up in "The Cloud," in *The Ebony Tower*. Death is not "at all being unable to escape the present; but being all the futures, all the pasts, being yesterday and tomorrow; which left today like a fragile grain between two implacable and immense millstones."

14. See Benjamin Lee Whorf's report on the temporal world of the Hopi Indians, "An American Indian Model of the Universe," in *Language, Thought and Reality* (New York: Wiley; London, Chapman & Hall, 1956).

15. *Time in Literature* (Berkeley: University of California Press, 1955), p. 118.

16. Ibid., pp. 109–10.

17. The fork is a recurring motif in Fowles's fiction. The temporal pattern of the novels comes to approach what Jorge Luis Borges once described in "The Garden of Forking Paths" as a "growing, dizzying net of divergent, converging and parallel times." *Labyrinths* (New York: New Directions, 1962), p. 55.

18. Friedrich Kümmel discusses space, time, and reality in Greek thought in "Time as Succession and the Problem of Duration," in *The Voices of Time*, ed. J. T. Fraser (London: Penguin, 1968).

19. See Jacqueline de Romily, *Time in Greek Tragedy* (Ithaca N.Y.: Cornell University Press, 1968).

20. See J. T. Fraser, *Of Time, Passion, and Knowledge* (New York: George Braziller, 1975).

21. See ibid., pp. 303–4.

22. Ibid., p. 304.

23. As I have pointed out in the introduction, it is the clash of incompatible cognitive repertoires that produces the eerie, the uncanny, the ambiguous. Humor is just about the only way of avoiding this type of sensation. Fowles gets his best effects by *not* using humor. When he does the Fowlesian "atmosphere" is gone.

24. Bertram Park, *Collins Guide to Roses* (London: Collins, 1969), p. 106.

25. In the first British edition (Cape) this statement is made on page 180, and Green there discusses a fictional or fictive time-span of "one hundred and eighty pages at least." In the first American edition (Little, Brown & Co.) the passage is to be found on page 183, and Green there refers, of course, to "one hundred and eighty-three pages at least." This again emphasizes the status of the page as a unit of time in *Mantissa*.

26. See note 3.

27. See S. J. Dimond and J. G. Beaumont, eds., *Hemisphere Function in the Human Brain* (London: Elek, 1974) and M. Corballis and I. L. Beale, *The Psychology of Left and Right* (Hillsdale, New Jersey: Lawrence Erlbaum Associates, 1976).

28. From Latin *dexter*, right; and *laevus*, left. My argument, here, is that "logical," serial time is the temporal expression of a cognitive submechanism closely associated with verbalization; holotemporality (or dextrotemporality), on the other hand, is a more free-wheeling human sense of time less closely associated with the cerebral left of the verbally dominant hemisphere. This theory would seem to receive support from lines of thought separating cognitive specialization and emotional holism in Roger Sperry's Nobel lecture (Stockholm 8 December 1981). Inner experience is not a kind of quaint end-product; instead it has an integral causal control role in brain function and behavior: "The more structured and specific informational components of cognitive processing were shown to be separable from the emotional and connotational components. The former remained confined within the hemisphere in which it was generated, whereas the emotional overtones leaked across to influence neural processing in the other hemisphere. The evidence of this separability is in itself significant in regard to questions of the organization of the neural mechanisms of cognition. . . . The results add up to a fundamental change in what science has long stood for throughout the materialist-behaviorist era." "Some Effects of Disconnecting the Cerebral Hemispheres," *Science* 217 (24 September 1982), 1226.

29. J. G. Beaumont and S. J. Dimond, eds., *Hemisphere Function in the Human Brain* (London: Elek, 1974), pp. 111–12.

30. "Another broadly relevant outcome . . . is a growing recognition of, and respect for, the inherent individuality in the structure of human intellect. The more we learn, the more we recognize the unique complexity of any one individual intellect and the stronger the conclusion becomes that the individuality inherent in our brain networks makes that of fingerprints or facial features gross and simple by comparison." See note 10.

31. From *The Invisible Writing* (1954), reprinted in Arthur Koestler, *Bricks to Babel* (London: Hutchinson, 1980; Picador/Pan Books, 1982), pp. 138–40.

Select Bibliography

1. Major Works by John Fowles

The Aristos: A Self-Portrait in Ideas. Boston: Little, Brown & Co., 1964; London: Cape, 1965; first rev. ed., with preface London: Pan Books, 1968; first rev. American ed., with extended preface, New York: New American Library/Signet, 1970; second rev. ed., with further preface extension, London: Cape, 1980.

The Collector. London: Cape, 1963; Boston: Little, Brown & Co., 1963.

Daniel Martin. London: Cape, 1977; Boston: Little, Brown & Co., 1977.

The Ebony Tower. London: Cape, 1974; Boston: Little, Brown & Co., 1974.

The Enigma of Stonehenge. London: Cape, 1980; New York: Summit Books, 1980.

The French Lieutenant's Woman. London: Cape, 1969; Boston: Little, Brown & Co., 1969; limited and signed ed., with special message, Franklin Center, Penn.: The Franklin Library, 1979.

Islands. London: Cape, 1978; Boston: Little, Brown & Co., 1978.

The Magus. Boston: Little, Brown & Co., 1965; London: Cape, 1966.

The Magus: A Revised Version, with Foreword. London: Cape, 1977; Boston: Little, Brown & Co., 1978.

Mantissa. London: Cape, 1982; Boston: Little, Brown & Co., 1982.

Poems. New York: Ecco Press, 1973; Toronto: Macmillan, 1973.

Shipwreck. London: Cape, 1974; Boston: Little, Brown & Co., 1975.

The Tree. London: Aurum Press, 1979; Boston: Little, Brown & Co., 1980.

2. Essays by John Fowles: A Selection

"Hardy and the Hag." In *Thomas Hardy after Fifty Years,* edited by Lance St. John Butler. London: Macmillan, 1977.

"Is the Novel Dead?" *Books* 1 (Autumn 1970): 2–5.

"Jacqueline Kennedy Onassis and Other First (and Last) Ladies." *Cosmopolitan* (October 1970): 144–49.

"*The Magus* Revisited." *London Times,* 28 May 1977, p. 7.

"Making a Pitch for Cricket." *Sports Illustrated,* 21 May 1973: 100–103.

"My Recollections of Kafka." *Mosaic* (Summer 1970): 31–41.

"Notes on Writing a Novel." *Harper's Magazine* 237 (July 1968): 88–97.

"Of Memoirs and Magpies." *Atlantic* 235 (June 1975): 82–84.

"On Being English but Not British." *Texas Quarterly* 7 (Autumn 1964): 154–62.

"Party of One: The Trouble with Starlets." *Holiday* 39 (June 1966): 12–20.

"Remembering Cruikshank." *Library Chronicle* 35 (1973), xiii–xvi.

"Seeing Nature Whole." *Harper's Magazine* 259 (November 1979): 49–68.

"Weeds, Bugs, Americans." *Sports Illustrated,* 21 December 1970: 84–88.

3. Books with Foreword or Afterword by John Fowles

Alain-Fournier, Henri. *The Wanderer* (*Le Grand Meaulnes,* 1913). Translated by Lowell Bair. New York: New American Library/Signet, 1971.

Baring-Gould, Sabine. *Mehalah: A Story of the Salt Marshes* (1880). Reprinted, London: Chatto & Windus, 1969.

Brendon, Piers. *Hawker of Morwenstow: Portrait of a Victorian Eccentric.* London: Cape, 1975.

Clark, Philip; Jackman, Brian; and Mercer, Derrick, eds. *The Sunday Times Book of the Countryside:* London and Sydney, 1980.

Doyle, Sir Arthur Conan. *The Hound of the Baskervilles* (1902). Reprinted, London: Murray & Cape, 1974.

Etudes sur "The French Lieutenant's Woman" de John Fowles. Caen: Annales du Centre Régional de Documentation Pédagogique de Caen, 1977.

Jefferies, Richard. *After London or Wild England.* Oxford: Oxford Univ. Press, 1980.

Mahfouz, Naguib. *Mirmar.* Cairo: Heinemann, 1978.

Marie de France. *The Lais of Marie de France.* Translated by Robert Hanning and Joan Ferrante. New York: E. P. Dutton, 1978.

4. Translations by John Fowles

Durfort, Clarie de. *Ourika* (1824). Austin, Texas: W. Thomas Taylor, 1977.

Perrault, Charles. *Cendrillon* (1697), adapted as *Cinderella:* London: Cape, 1974; Boston: Little, Brown & Co., 1976.

5. Descriptive Introductions to John Fowles

Huffaker, Robert Selwyn. *John Fowles.* Boston: Twayne, 1980.

Olshen, Barry. *John Fowles.* New York: Frederick Ungar, 1978.

————, and Olshen, Toni. *John Fowles: A Reference Guide.* Boston: G. K. Hall & Co., 1980.

Palmer, William J. *The Fiction of John Fowles: Tradition, Art, and the Loneliness of Selfhood.* Columbia: University of Missouri Press, 1974.

Wolfe, Peter. *John Fowles: Magus and Moralist.* Lewisburg, Pa.: Bucknell University Press, 1976; London: Associated University Presses, 1976.

6. Books with Criticism on John Fowles

Alter, Robert. *Partial Magic: The Novel as a Self-Conscious Genre.* Berkeley: University of California Press, 1975.

Bergonzi, Bernard. *The Situation of the Novel.* Pittsburgh, Pa.: University of Pittsburgh Press; London: Macmillan, 1970.

Bradbury, Malcolm. *Possibilities: Essays on the State of the Novel.* London: Oxford University Press, 1973.

Hayman, Ronald. *The Novel Today, 1967–1975.* London: Longman, 1976.

Higdon, David Leon. *Time and English Fiction.* London: Macmillan, 1977.

Karl, Frederick R. *A Reader's Guide to the Contemporary English Novel.* New York: Farrar, Straus & Giroux; London: Thames & Hudson, 1972.

Kennedy, Alan. *The Protean Self: Dramatic Action in Contemporary Fiction.* London: Macmillan; New York: Columbia University Press, 1974.

Lodge, David. *Working with Structuralism: Essays and Reviews on Nineteenth and Twentieth-Century Literature.* Boston, London, and Henley: Routledge & Kegan Paul, 1981.

Morris, Robert K., ed. *Old Lines, New Forces: Essays on the Contemporary British Novel, 1960–1970.* London: Associated University Presses, 1976.

Scholes, Robert. *Fabulation and Meta-Fiction.* Urbana: University of Illinois Press, 1979.

————. *Structuralism in Literature: An Introduction.* New Haven, Conn.: Yale University Press, 1974.

7. Essays on John Fowles: A Selection

Adam, Ian; Brantlinger, Patrick; and Rothblatt, Sheldon. "*The French Lieutenant's Woman:* A Discussion." *Victorian Studies* 15 (March 1972): 339–56.

Begnal, Michael H. "A View of John Fowles' *The Magus.*" *Modern British Literature* 3 (Fall 1978): 67–72.

Berets, Ralph. "*The Magus:* A Study in the Creation of a Personal Myth." *Twentieth Century Literature* 19 (April 1973): 89–98.

Binns, Ronald. "John Fowles: Radical Romancer." *Critical Quarterly* 15 (Winter 1973): 317–34.

Churchill, Thomas. "Waterhouse, Storey, and Fowles: Which Way Out of the Room?" *Critique* 10 (Summer 1968): 72–87.

Costa, Richard Hauer. "Trickery's Mixed Bag: The Perils of Fowles' *French Lieutenant's Woman.*" *Rocky Mountain Review of Language and Literature* 29 (Spring 1975): 1–9.

Detweiler, Robert. "The Unity of John Fowles' Fiction." *Notes on Contemporary Literature* 1 (March 1971): 3–4.

DeVitis, A. A., and Palmer, William J. "*A Pair of Blue Eyes* Flash at *The French Lieutenant's Woman.*" *Contemporary Literature* 15 (Winter 1974): 90–101.

Eddins, Dwight. "John Fowles: Existence as Authorship." *Contemporary Literature* 17 (Spring 1976): 204–22.

Evarts, Prescott, Jr. "Fowles' *The French Lieutenant's Woman* as Tragedy." *Critique* 13 (1972): 57–69.

Fleishman, Avrom. "*The Magus* of the Wizard of the West." *Journal of Modern Literature* 5 (April 1976): 297–314.

Gindin, James. "Three Recent British Novels and an American Response." *Michigan Quarterly Review* 17 (Spring 1978): 223–46.

Gordon, Jan B. "Prisons of Consciousness in Contemporary European Fiction." *Southern Review* 9 (Winter 1973): 217–32.

Gross, David. "Historical Consciousness and the Modern Novel: The Uses of History in the Fiction of John Fowles." *Studies in the Humanities* 7 (December 1978): 19–27.

Kane, Patricia. "The Fallen Woman as Free-Thinker in *The French Lieutenant's Woman* and *The Scarlet Letter.*" *Notes on Contemporary Literature* 2 (1972): 8–10.

Laughlin, Rosemary M. "Faces of Power in the Novels of John Fowles." *Critique* 13 (1972): 71–88.

Lindblad, Ishrat. " 'La Bonne Vaux,' 'la Princesse Lointaine'—Two Motifs in the Novels of John Fowles." In *Studies in English Philology, Linguistics and Literature Presented to Alarik Rynell, 7 March 1978*, edited by Mats Rydén and Lennart A. Björk. *Stockholm Studies in English* 46 (1978): 87–101.

Presley, Delma E. "The Quest of the Bourgeois Hero: An Approach to Fowles's *The Magus.*" *Journal of Popular Culture* 6 (Fall 1972): 394–98.

Rankin, Elizabeth D. "Cryptic Coloration in *The French Lieutenant's Woman.*" *Journal of Narrative Technique* 3 (September 1973): 193–207.

Rose, Gilbert J. "*The French Lieutenant's Woman:* The Unconscious Significance of a Novel to Its Author." *American Imago* 29 (Summer 1972): 165–76.

Rubenstein, Roberta. "Myth, Mystery, and Irony: John Fowles's *The Magus.*" *Contemporary Literature* 16 (Summer 1975): 328–39.

Scholes, Robert. "The Orgastic Fiction of John Fowles." *Hollins Critic* 6 (December 1969): 1–12.

8. Works on Time

Alexander, Samuel. *Space, Time and Deity.* London: Macmillan, 1934.

Bergson, Henri. *Time and Free Will.* New York: MacMillan & Co., 1910.

Block, Richard A. "Time and Consciousness" in *Aspects of Consciousness* (eds. G. Underwood and R. Stevens). London and New York: Academic Press, 1979.

Burke, Peter. *The Renaissance Sense of the Past.* New York: St. Martin's Press, 1969.

Callahan, John. *Four Views of Time in Ancient Philosophy.* Cambridge, Mass.: Harvard University Press, 1948.

Church, Margaret. *Time and Reality: Studies in Contemporary Fiction.* Chapel Hill: University of North Carolina Press, 1949.

Cullmann, Oscar. *Christ and Time: The Primitive Christian Conception of Time and History.* Translated by Floyd V. Filson. Philadelphia: Westminster Press, 1964; London: SCM Press, 1967.

Denbigh, Kenneth G. *An Inventive Universe.* London: Hutchinson & Co., 1975.

Doob, Leonard W. *Patterning of Time.* New Haven and London: Yale University Press, 1971.

Efron, Robert. "Temporal Perception, Aphasia and Déjà Vu," *Brain* 86 (1965): 403–24.

Fisher, R., ed. "Interdisciplinary Perspectives of Time." *Annals of the New York Academy of Science* 138, art. 2 (1967).

Fraser, J. T. *The Genesis and Evolution of Time: A Critique of Interpretation in Physics.* Amherst: University of Mass. Press, 1982; Brighton: Harvester Press, 1982.

————. *Of Time, Passion, and Knowledge: Reflections on the Strategy of Existence.* New York: George Braziller, 1975.

————. *Time as Conflict: A Scientific and Humanistic Study.* Basel and Boston: Birkhauser, 1978.

————. ed. *The Voices of Time: A Comparative Survey of Man's Views of Time as Expressed by the Sciences and the Humanities.* 1966; 2nd. ed. Amherst: University of Massachusetts Press, 1981.

————. Lawrence, N.; and Park, D., eds. *The Study of Time III: Proceedings of the Third Conference of the International Society for the Study of Time.* New York and Heidelberg: Springer-Verlag, 1978.

Grünbaum, Adolf. *Philosophical Problems of Space and Time.* New York: Knopf, 1963.

————. "The Status of Temporal Becoming." *Annals of the New York Academy of Science,* 138, art. 2: (1967).

Gunn, J. Alexander. *The Problem of Time: An Historical and Critical Study.* London: Allen & Unwin, 1929.

Heidegger, Martin. *Being and Time.* Translated by J. Macquarrie and E. Robinson. London: SCM Press, 1962.

Kubler, George. *The Shape of Time: Remarks on the History of Things.* New Haven, Conn.: Yale University Press, 1962.

Kümmel. Friedrich. "Time as Succession and the Problem of Duration." Translated by Francesco Gaona. In *The Voices of Time,* edited by J. T. Fraser. 1966; 2nd. ed. Amherst: University of Massachusetts Press, 1981.

Lewis, Wyndham. *Time and Western Man.* London: Chatto & Windus, 1927; New York: Harcourt, 1928.

Mendilow, A. A. *Time and the Novel.* New York: Humanities Press, 1972; first published 1952.

Meyerhoff, Hans. *Time in Literature.* Berkeley and Los Angeles: University of California Press, 1955.

Minkowski, Eugène. *Le temps vécu.* Paris: Collection de L'Evolution Psychiatrique, 1933.

Ornstein, Robert. *On the Experience of Time.* London: Pelican, 1975; first published 1969.

Polzella, J. Donald; DaPolito, Frank; and Hinsman, Christine M. "Cerebral Asymmetry in Time Perception." *Perception and Psychophysics* 21 (1977): 187–92.

Poulet, Georges. *Studies in Human Time.* Translated by E. Coleman. New York: Harper and Row, 1956.

Raleigh, John H. *Time, Place and Idea: Essays on the Novel.* Carbondale: Southern Illinois University Press, 1968.

Ridley, B. K. *Time, Space and Things.* Harmondsworth: Penguin, 1976.

Romily, Jacqueline de. *Time in Greek Tragedy.* Ithaca, N.Y.: Cornell University Press, 1968.

Schaltenbrand, Georges. "Consciousness and Time." *New York Academy of Science* 138 (1967): 632–45.

Sherover, Charles M. *The Human Experience of Time: The Development of Its Philosophic Meaning.* New York: New York University Press, 1975.

Spencer, Sharon. *Space, Time, and Structure in the Modern Novel.* New York: New York University Press, 1971.

Thomas, Ewart A. C., and Weaver, Wanda B. "Cognitive Processing and Time Perception." *Perception and Psychophysics* 17 (1975): 363–67.

Tobin, Patricia D. *Time and the Novel: The Genealogical Imperative.* Princeton, N.J.: Princeton University Press, 1978.

9. Other Works

Barrett, William. *Time of Need: Forms of Imagination in the Twentieth Century.* New York, Evanston, San Francisco; London: Harper & Row, 1972.

Barthes, Roland. *Mythologies.* Paris: Seuil, 1970; first ed. 1953.

———. *Le Plaisir du texte.* Paris: Seuil, 1973.

Beaumont, J. G., and Dimond, S. J., eds. *Hemisphere Function in the Human Brain.* London: Elek, 1974.

Ben-Dov, Gita, and Carmon, Amiram. "On Time, Space, and the Cerebral Hemispheres: A Theoretical Note." *International Journal of Neuroscience* 7 (1976): 29–33.

Brabyn, Howard. "Mother Tongue and the Brain." *Unesco Courier,* February 1982.

Bruner, Jerome. *On Knowing: Essays for the Left Hand.* Cambridge, Mass.: Harvard University Press, 1962.

Corballis, Michael C., and Beale, Ivan L. *The Psychology of Left and Right.* Hillsdale, New Jersey: Lawrence Erlbaum Associates, 1976.

Culler, Jonathan. *Structuralist Poetics: Structuralism, Linguistics and the Study of Literature.* London: Routledge & Kegan Paul, 1975.

Derrida, Jacques. *La Dissémination.* Paris: Seuil, 1972.

———. *L'Ecriture et la différence.* Paris: Seuil, 1967.

Fischer, Roland. "A Cartography of the Ecstatic and Meditative States." *Science* 174 (1971): 897–904.

Foucault, Michel. *L'Archéologie du savoir.* Paris: Gallimard, 1969.

Fromm, Erich. *Greatness and Limitations of Freud's Thought.* New York: Harper & Row, 1980.

———. *The Sane Society.* London: George Allen & Unwin, 1957.

Gamma, Karl. *The Handbook of Skiing.* London: Dorling Kindersley, 1981.

Gardner, Martin. *The Ambidextrous Universe: Mirror Asymmetry and Time-Reversed Worlds*. New York: Charles Scribner's Sons, 1964; rpt. 1979.

Gazzaniga, Michael S. *The Bisected Brain*. New York: Appleton-Century-Crofts, 1970.

———, and LeDoux, J. E. *The Integrated Mind*. New York and London: Plenum Press, 1978.

Geschwind, Norman, and Behan, Peter. "Left-Handedness: Association with Immune Disease, Migraine, and Developmental Learning Disorder." *Proceedings of the National Academy of Science*. Vol. 79, pp. 5097–100, August 1982.

Gooch, Stan. "Right Brain, Left Brain." *New Scientist*. 11 September, 1980, pp. 790–92.

Hadamard, J. *The Psychology of Invention in the Mathematical Field*. Princeton, N.J.: Princeton University Press, 1949.

Heath, Stephen. *The Nouveau Roman: A Study in the Practice of Writing*. London: Elek, 1972.

Koestler, Arthur. *The Act of Creation*. London: Hutchinson, 1964.

———. *Bricks to Babel: Selected Writings with Comments by the Author*. London: Hutchinson, 1980.

———. *The Ghost in the Machine*. London: Hutchinson, 1967.

Lacan, Jacques. *Ecrits*. Paris: Seuil, 1966.

LeDoux, Joseph E. "Neuroevolutionary Mechanisms of Cerebral Asymmetry in Man." *Brain, Behaviour, and Evolution* 20 (1982): 196–212.

Lentricchia, Frank. *After the New Criticism*. Chicago: University of Chicago Press; London: Athlone Press, 1980.

Lévi-Strauss, Claude. *Le Cru et le cuit*. Paris: Plon, 1964.

———. *La Pensée sauvage*. Paris: Plon, 1962.

McLellan, David, *The Thought of Karl Marx*. London: Macmillan, 1971.

———. *Marx's Grundrisse*. London: Macmillan, 1971.

Macpherson, C. B. *The Real World of Democracy*. Canadian Broadcasting Corporation, 1965; Oxford: Clarendon Press, 1966; New York: Oxford University Press, 1972.

Marx, Karl. *Economic and Philosophic Manuscripts of 1844*. Translated by Dirk J. Struik. New York: International Publishers, 1964.

Needham, Rodney, ed. *Right and Left: Essays on Dual Symbolic Classification*. Chicago: University of Chicago Press, 1973.

Park, Bertram. *Collins Guide to Roses*. London: Collins, 1956.

Pollio, Howard R. "Intuitive Thinking." In *Aspects of Consciousness I* (eds. Geoffrey Underwood and Robin Stevens). London and New York: Academic Press, 1979.

Porac, Clare, and Coren, Stanley. *Lateral Preferences and Human Behavior*. New York, Heidelberg, Berlin: Springer-Verlag, 1981.

Sanders, Scott. "The Left-Handedness of Modern Literature." *Twentieth Century Literature* 23, no. 4 (December 1977): 417–36.

Schmidt, Robert F., ed. *Fundamentals of Neurophysiology*. Translated by M. A. Biederman-Thorson. 2nd ed. New York, Heidelberg, Berlin: Springer-Verlag, 1978.

Sperry, Roger, W. *Science and Moral Priority: Merging Mind, Brain, and Human Values*. New York: Columbia Univ. Press, 1983.

———. "Some Effects of Disconnecting the Cerebral Hemispheres." *Science* 217 (September 1982): 1223–26. (The Nobel lecture: Stockholm, 8 December 1981.)

Todorov, Tzvetan. *Littérature et signification*. Paris: Larousse, 1967.

———. *Poétique de la prose*. Paris: Seuil, 1971.

Underwood, Geoffrey, and Stevens, Robin (eds.). *Aspects of Consciousness I*. London and New York: Academic Press, 1979.

Whorf, B. L. *Language, Thought and Reality*. New York: Wiley; London: Chapman & Hall, 1956.

Young, Robert. *Untying the Text: A Post-Structuralist Reader*. London: Routledge & Kegan Paul, 1981.

Index